Never Say Never

Never Say Never

Finding a Life That Fits

Ricki Lake

with

Rebecca DiLiberto

ATRIA BOOKS

New York London Toronto Sydney New Delhi

ATRIA BOOKS

A Division of Simon & Schuster, Inc.
1230 Avenue of the Americas
New York, NY 10020

First Atria Books hardcover edition April 2012

ATRIA BOOKS and colophon are trademarks of Simon & Schuster, Inc.

For information about special discounts for bulk purchases, please contact Simon & Schuster Special Sales at 1-866-506-1949 or business@simonandschuster.com.

The Simon & Schuster Speakers Bureau can bring authors to your live event. For more information or to book an event, contact the Simon & Schuster Speakers Bureau at 1-866-248-3049 or visit our website at www.simonspeakers.com.

Designed by Suet Chong

Manufactured in the United States of America

10 9 8 7 6 5 4 3 2 1

Library of Congress Cataloging-in-Publication Data

Lake, Ricki.
  Never say never : finding a life that fits / by Ricki Lake; with Rebecca DiLiberto. — 1st Atria Books hardcover ed.
      p.   cm.
1. Lake, Ricki.   2. Television personalities—United States—Biography.
I. DiLiberto, Rebecca.   II. Title.
  PN1992.4.L26A3   2012
  791.4502'8092—dc23
  [B]   2012006638

ISBN 978-1-4516-2718-3
ISBN 978-1-4516-2719-0 (ebook)

For Christian

*Never allow a person to tell you no
who doesn't have the power to say yes.*

—ELEANOR ROOSEVELT

Foreword

John Waters

Let's get this right out of the way. I love Ricki Lake fat, thin, chubby, rich, poor, single, dating, married, divorced, engaged again; I love Ricki even when I have to watch her give birth in a bathtub in *The Business of Being Born*. I guess that is unconditional love. She's not only been in four of my movies (*Hairspray, Cry-Baby, Serial Mom*, and *Cecil B. DeMented*), she's my buddy too. The teenage girl who helped me move over to the mainstream (at least for a while) became *the* friend who knows my private life and continues to keep reinventing herself and dragging me along with her by our filmic association. Yep, that was me as a "surprise" guest on the *Ricki's Baby Shower* episode of her TV series, and yeah, I did pop in unannounced (with a network TV crew!) to Ricki's dance rehearsal with partner Derek Hough to offer them some advice for *Dancing with the Stars*. "Put a little S&M in the dance routines," I urged; a line which was, of course, cut out once the show aired. Ricki shoulda won that show, not come in second, much less third! I tried to give her other pointers too. Since *Hairspray* the world already knew Ricki could dance, and that she really wasn't fat anymore, how could she become an underdog again to appeal more to the home voters? "Get pimples," I suggested. "Run off with Chaz.

Have a health scare—maybe an outbreak of goiters? Punch Nancy Grace."

But Ricki Lake doesn't need my advice. She can't help herself—she's somehow an insider even when acting like an outsider, and always appeals to a larger minority than I ever could. Once, at the height of her TV fame, Ricki and I were trapped in an airport for eight hours together due to weather-related cancelled flights. Every black person recognized her and every steward recognized me. You do the numbers.

Her publisher ought to be thrilled by this book because she reveals a lot inside! Being dumped. Cruising online for dates. Big cocks. Hideous divorces. There's even stuff I didn't know. Being sexually abused by the family's handyman as a child. (It makes me think of Rhoda Penmark, the homicidal child in *The Bad Seed*, and how she set her handyman on fire; Ricki should have done the same.) Or having to watch a porn movie as a chubby, teen actress on an audition with a creepy, pervert producer. I certainly didn't know she ever had a problem with drugs. I never even saw Ricki smoke pot. But Ambien? Christ, I would have told her about "black beauties," the scary diet pills I used to take as a skinny teen for kicks, if I knew she wanted to get high!

If I were a shrink, Ricki would be my happiest patient—despite the fact she doesn't speak to her mother. True, in the past she has dated like a gay man trapped in a woman's body, but as she confides, "What actress's first boyfriend *wasn't* gay?" I'd get her to concentrate on what I see as her only neurosis: paying for too much stuff for all her past beaus. Let them treat you to McDonald's if that's all they can afford and then fuck them in the bathroom if you need to show your appreciation. I think it's healthy she admits to being horny and responding

well, sexually, to "kind firmness." What control freak (and everyone in show-biz is) doesn't want to give it up a little—be told
what to do? As her closet psychiatrist, I'd want her to wonder
why she never had a chubby-chaser partner, or that maybe they
all were and she never realized it. I know there are guys who
"knead" the love of a big-boned gal, and at her heaviest, Ricki
would have been a goddess for many. Of course I'd watch the
limits of her playful masochism and make sure she doesn't find
a "feeder"—sadist types who encourage overeating in their already fat partners—until they are so heavy they can't get out of
the bed unless Richard Simmons shows up to hoist them out of
the second floor windows with a crane. Don't laugh. Ricki's had
some crazy boyfriends. Who hasn't?

   If Ricki thinks of Divine as her movie mom, I hope I can
still be her movie dad. I look back on our early days together and
it's like seeing a family scrapbook. Ah, *Hairspray*—Ricki shopping for junk food in the supermarket in Baltimore after shooting, still wearing her real peroxide-heavy hair ratted up "like
a teenage Jezebel" just because I wanted to be authentic and
avoid wigs. Proving her cinematic chops by allowing me to put
live roaches in her bouffant for a scene that was later cut. And
of course, the "fat continuity" problem on *Hairspray* we never
expected—Ricki losing so much weight because of dance rehearsals that the crew had to feed her Dove bars between takes
so her weight would match a shot filmed earlier. Was it wrong
of me to conspire with her mom, who was very normal, nice
(to me), and still Jewish at the time, to not tell Ricki that her
grandfather died until we finished that week's shooting, so we
could schedule her grief? Sometimes even cinematic dads make
questionable decisions.

Yes, Ricki, you've gone through a lot, but I'm proud that you've never whined about being famous. We both know that when something bad happens in your personal life and you're in show business, you're lucky—you can still use it financially. Bad men give you new chapters. A painful divorce is a story arc and like all "high concept" movies, you need three acts; you had something, you lost it, and you got it back and learned. Tragedy, if you are well known to the public, is just fresh material, but in real life, if you don't have an artistic outlet—it's called misery.

I secretly save all your tabloid headlines even though I know they can make you crazy. I remember how pissed off you were when one rag published stills of you from *Cry-Baby*, in character, as an eight-month pregnant teen with a prosthetic stomach, claiming this was a real-life photo of you at the very fattest you had ever been. Just last week you were on the cover of all three of the trash papers with conflicting stories about your weight: "Ricki's Guy Likes Her Chubby," "Ricki's Desperate to Drop Another Twenty Pounds," and "Too Fat for Wedding Dress." I'm jealous. No journalist ever cared about my weight.

As a loving friend, what I wish for you most is that you don't forget your acting career. You are really good! Go ahead, have a bestseller! Another hit TV series! A brand new, happy marriage! But please don't forget the next generation of crazy filmmakers who need to have you in their movies. I want you back on the silver screen, where you belong.

I'll never get cast as the ingenue.
I'll never be kissed in real life.
This movie will never be a hit.
I'll never fall in love.
I'll never need to work again.
I'll never work again.
I'll never get this talk show gig.
I'll never last more than a season.
I'll never get married.
I'll never get divorced.
I'll never leave New York.
I'll never leave my husband.
I'll never date again.
I'll never date online.
I'll never fall for that trick.
I'll never fall in love again.
I'll never do another talk show.
I'll never get married again.
I'll never do *Dancing with the Stars*.
I'll never forgive my enemies.
I'll never be satisfied.
NEVER SAY NEVER.

I'll never be happy unless I come in first.

If you had told me my entire life's trajectory would hinge on my abilities as a dancer, I would never have believed you. But this book begins with a fat girl winning a dance contest and ends with a much thinner woman coming in third. Both of those people were me. And while I'm the first to admit that winning can sometimes mean everything, I can honestly say that this time, it felt really great being a loser.

Introduction

Three days before I performed live for the first time on *Dancing with the Stars* in the fall of 2011, I stared into the floor-to-ceiling mirror in the dance studio where I'd been training with my partner, ballroom pro Derek Hough, and tried not to hyperventilate. Had I really decided to attempt to learn to dance on national television, wearing a sequined bathing suit? Was I hallucinating? Was there a loophole I could crawl my way out of? *Does somebody have a copy of my contract?*

I wasn't worried about whether I would be able to pick up the complicated dance steps. I wasn't worried about going back on TV in front of millions of viewers after such a long hiatus. I wasn't worried about performing well enough to keep my spot on the show.

I was worried about looking fat.

Even after twenty years of slaying my demons, I was still most concerned with how I looked. When a professional dancer sees her own reflection, she's not looking for double chins or figure flaws; she's studying lines, steps, and timing. The relationship between a dancer and her mirror image isn't about emotions or self-punishment; the mirror is simply a crucial tool that promotes her progress when it is used correctly. Most of us try to avoid confrontations with our reflections whenever possible, seeing the looking glass as the enemy. The dancer calls the mirror her friend and teacher.

But when I catch a glimpse of myself in a store window, I quickly avert my gaze.

Staring at my hips in the mirror, in an effort to make them move like a dancer's, was awkward for me, plain and simple. The very first day we worked together, Derek commanded me to stare down my own image and truly believe, deep down in my gut, that I was a beautiful dancer. Only if I was able to do this, he said, would it become true. I knew that he was right, but I doubted that I'd ever be so confident.

The first week of the show, I pushed past my fears and strutted out onto that dance floor in a skintight dress. I danced pretty darn well for a girl with no ballroom experience, earning high marks and tons of applause. But my performance didn't really impress me. The thing I was most proud of was getting a little bit thinner.

I'm not comfortable being a role model. I'm well aware that what works for me does not necessarily work for everyone else. And I find nothing to be less helpful to my own personal growth and development than having to listen to some well-known person preach about how good he or she is at doing something really, really hard—something that people all over the world are struggling with. What's more discouraging than being told that someone else has found the answer to a dilemma you've never been able to solve? It just makes you feel like even more of a failure.

Take what many refer to as my weight-loss "success."

Instead of thinking of my shape shifting as a success—

something I've already accomplished—I see staying fit as more of a process. It's a practice that will never come to an end—meditation for the body rather than the mind. Controlling my weight requires compromise and sacrifice, but I don't mind the ongoing effort to keep my body healthy and comfortable—a place I actually want to live in. In fact, I feel lucky to have the strength, stamina, and support to keep improving my physical condition and the capacity to forgive myself when I slip up and gain a few pounds. I've finally accepted that there's no such thing as "finished" when it comes to being fit. Even the most immaculate house requires regular cleaning, and you have to keep training your muscles and appetite in order not to lose ground in your fitness battle.

I am so far from being "perfect" (thank God for that—"perfect" people bug the shit out of me) that it amazes me whenever anyone asks me for advice. I've made so many mistakes. Perhaps you're familiar with one or two of them? Maybe you noticed my name while you were scanning the tabloids in the grocery checkout line. I've gone on crash diets. I've tried crazy exercise regimens. Once, while working on a film, I ate so little in my effort to slim down that I became dehydrated and was forced to check into the hospital until my blood chemistries stabilized. In the film I was working on, I was playing the role of a cancer patient, and I was doing my best to look like one. Sick. I still get just as desperate and insecure about my body as anyone else, even though I achieved what many call a weight-loss milestone many years ago when I lost over 100 pounds.

When I talk about my experiences with weight loss and the transformation, inside and out, that can result from it, I'm not presenting myself as an expert. I'm trying to offer solidarity and maybe an insight or two. This book is my effort to be totally candid and honest about my experience gaining, then losing, and finally recapturing control of my own body.

First and foremost, there was no one magical moment—no trick, no fluke of chemistry or psychology. Many things came into play that enabled me to finally feel empowered, rather than hopeless, when it came to my weight. It was a perfect storm of need, luck, and determination.

I credit my initial weight loss to sheer professional desperation: I needed to work, and I was too fat for anyone to hire me. My career as the lovable fat chick had run its course, and executives and audiences needed something new to market. So I lost all my money, went into hiding, starved myself, worked my butt off, and scored my very own talk show.

But that initial transformation was only the beginning. Like all other people who have difficulty controlling their weight, I've been up and down the scale for most of my life, and it's only now, at the age of forty-three, that I honestly think the worst of my struggles may be behind me. (I do hope that writing that down doesn't jinx things!)

The reason for this change? For the first time in my life, I've been given the honor of feeling truly unconditional love.

I'm not talking about "love" in some vague, spiritual sense. I'm talking about hot, sexy, uncompromising, passionate, emotional, terrifying, gratifying, mind-blowing human love. Love from a gorgeous man, for both what's inside me and what I look like on the outside. From the first time I went to bed with my fiancé, Christian, I realized I had never truly known what it was like to be inside myself experiencing real pleasure—the kind of pleasure that unifies the body, mind, and spirit in passion and total care for another human being. I'd always been watching myself from outside—acting out the experience of pleasure without truly feeling it.

Since the beginning of time, a woman has needed a man—in some form or another—to create human life. Even the creationists and the Darwinists have nothing to argue about on this one! In no way do I mean this to sound antifeminist, but I believe that I needed Christian's help in order to give birth to my truest, happiest self. We met each other at the wrong time in each of our lives to have a baby together, and for a while, this made me sad. But then I realized that Christian had already helped me to create a new life: my own.

If I could help women to achieve anything when it came to their bodies, it wouldn't be fitness or weight loss; it would be self-acceptance. I don't blame you if you're rolling your eyes right now: I would be too. People said it to me all my life, but I didn't really grasp the truth of the following statement until I experienced it myself: Unless you love yourself for who you are right now, you'll never become who you truly want to be. It may sound cheesy, it may sound paradoxical, but to me, it finally makes sense. Real, lasting change can't be negatively motivated; it has to be powered by positivity.

Before I met Christian, if you ever would have told me I'd agree to appear weekly on national television in skintight costumes, attempting complicated, athletic choreography in front of a live studio audience, I'd have said you were crazy.

"Never," I'd have replied.

But you know by now what I have to say about the word *never*: I've learned to never say it.

1

I'll never be anything special.

I grew up in a middle-class Jewish family in Hastings-on-Hudson, New York, a small town in Westchester County not far from Manhattan, but far enough away from the city that Manhattan always seemed like an exotic and magical place. We were the classic 1970s family of four. My father, Barry, worked as a pharmacist; my mother, Jill, was a stay-at-home mom; I was their firstborn; and my sister, Jennifer, came along just fourteen months after I did.

A few years ago, an interviewer for a parenting magazine asked me, "What's the best trick your mother ever taught you?"

"How to heat up a Hungry Man for dinner!" was my reply.

The person from whom I did get unconditional love was my father's mother, my Grandma Sylvia Lake. Doesn't the name sound as if it should belong to a famous person? It just belongs in lights:

"AND INTRODUCING . . . THE EFFERVESCENT SYLVIA LAKE!"

Grandma Sylvia was nothing short of a movie star to me. She looked like a cross between Patricia Neal and Gena Rowlands—all rosy cheeks and lipstick and glasses—the ultimate glamorous matriarch. Her hair was always "done," her jewelry always big. She seemed to give off some otherworldly light, since she positively glowed with energy and vibrance. Even though I was short and rotund, and the details of my everyday life were often gray and average, Grandma Sylvia taught me to look at the world through a rainbow-colored prism. (To a big thinker like Grandma Sylvia, rose-colored glasses are for amateur optimists.) Grandma Sylvia was always telling me that I was the smartest, the funniest, the prettiest. She called me "the most talented girl in the world," even when all I could do was half a cartwheel.

Grandma Sylvia shared her love of the arts with my sister, Jennifer, and me, taking us to the theater in Manhattan almost every weekend. I can still recall every spectacle I ever witnessed with her—from the opera to the ballet, *Annie* to *Pirates of Penzance*. I remember the way my heartbeat quickened as the house lights began to dim, the pit orchestra weaved together the first phrases of the overture, and the burgundy velvet curtain started to twitch, then glide its way open to reveal the magic behind it.

I can still conjure up the cozy feeling of grasping my grandmother's elegant, well-manicured hand with my squishy, miniature mitt as I settled into the seat. Going to the theater offered all the magic of my imagination except I didn't have to close my eyes. And though Grandma Sylvia and I were part of the audience, she always made me believe I was the star of the show.

My friends often tease me that I see the world through the eyes of a Disney princess, that I open my curtains each morning to savor the sweet smell of citrus trees and the music of songbirds. They're right—I kind of do.

No disrespect to Mr. Disney, but I inherited my sunny outlook from Grandma Sylvia, not some storybook princess. It was probably her positivity, both genetic and learned, that got me through her death from breast cancer in 1978, when she was only fifty-eight years old, and I was nine.

I still think of her every day because she was the person who enabled me to see the beauty in myself.

2

*I'll never let anybody find out
how much I weigh.*

⁓

While sashaying down Manhattan's Theatre Row with Grandma Sylvia was delightfully easy, being a chubby, average kid in Hastings-on-Hudson was not. Despite Grandma Sylvia's pep talks, I struggled with my self-esteem. Back in the seventies, teachers were not exactly aware of a child's negative or positive feelings about herself. Well, maybe they were conscious of their students' feelings, but (let's be honest) they weren't particularly concerned with more than teaching penmanship or drilling times tables. The goal of the grown-ups bringing up my generation was to raise successful kids, not happy ones. Perfection, not creativity, was valued. Harsh criticism was institutionalized. Those who thought well of themselves were punished, not rewarded. High self-esteem was viewed with the same disdain as arrogance.

Not that I needed to worry about seeming arrogant. I had been generously supplied—by fate, genetics, and those with whom I was forced to spend the majority of my time—with plenty of reasons to beat myself up. One particular memory highlights the horror that was elementary school gym class: a laboratory dedicated to the advancement of self-loathing, if ever there was one. I must have been on the cusp of finishing elementary school, at that awkward age when a kid looks and feels more like an undifferentiated blob of protoplasm than an adolescent on the verge of developing sexually. Although I didn't yet care about being attractive to boys, I was conscious of being heavier than everyone else in my class. I made every moment of my life into a "One of these things is not" situation. I was always comparing myself to the skinniest girls in school, and I assumed others were comparing me too. Looking back, I realize this must have been because of a family dynamic set up by my mother. Everything, especially weight, was a competition. Later in my life, I'm sure I stayed fat at least partly for the sake of pissing my mother off.

At the beginning of each school year, all the kids in the PE class had to line up in order of height and submit themselves to being weighed in front of a jury of their peers. Once you were weighed, it wasn't like at a Weight Watchers meeting, where some nice, skinny lady with sunken cheeks and too much makeup records your number in a secret book for no eyes but hers and your own.

Oh, no. This number was used as a tool of public shaming.

"BOBBY WHITE, 70 POUNDS!" the teacher would yell out to the back of the line, like a town crier.

"DEBORAH SMALL, 66!"

I don't know why our teacher needed to say the numbers out loud when she was already writing them down in a notebook for some mysterious auditor to consider. This is but one of the many mysteries that were part of a mundane suburban childhood in the 1970s, I suppose.

As I stood waiting my turn, I was a nervous wreck. My heart thumped in a wild rhythm, and sweat streamed down my forehead. Making my approach to the public scale was like walking the plank. I traveled there through invisible molasses, my limbs moving in slow motion, wanting to delay my judgment as long as possible. On the off-chance the world might end in the next minute or two, I wanted it to end before I'd been forced to suffer utter humiliation. Imagine if the last thing my entire class heard before surrendering their tiny, tragic souls to a fiery apocalypse was the astounding number of pounds I weighed!

Of course, I was never saved from that scale, by the bell, or the end of the world. As I stepped gingerly onto the Detecto, I remember marveling at how it could magically detect my fatness. I squeezed and tightened every muscle in my little body—a little body that, back in those days, felt way too big for me—as I stepped onto the machine that would forever measure precisely how different I was from everyone else.

For days before the dreaded weighing session, I expended a remarkable amount of brain power trying to find a way to trick the scale. *Would I weigh less if I placed only half my foot on the device's surface, and left the other dangling off?* Unfortunately not.

Tentatively I balanced on the scale, while the PE teacher fiddled with the dial sliding along the heavy aluminum beam. *Up-up-down-down-DOWN!-up-up. Enough already,* I thought, *Stop moving it for God's sake.*

"RICKI LAKE, 85 POUNDS!" the teacher screamed as she looked down to take note of my number. Even though I don't re-call any of the kids shouting out nasty comments, a cacophony of imaginary criticism echoed through my head as I bolted from the scale as fast as I could. My cheeks were flushed with em-barrassment. I felt supremely visible, frantic and puffed up like a marshmallow. I wanted to disappear. I wanted to forget the whole thing immediately.

I doubt any of my classmates remember the horror of gym class weigh-ins, blessed as they were not to have their own weight issues. It's so crazy how hang-ups are a big deal only when we give them the power to be that way. I'm sure there were at least a couple of other kids in my class who weighed as much as I did, but I was too busy feeling humiliated to notice.

The experience of measuring my own value inversely—*The less I weigh, the more I am worth*—was one I'd suffer through again and again throughout my life as an adult. And the feeling of being trapped in that gym class line still haunts me every time I catch myself trying to measure up to—or weigh in under—others.

I wasn't one of those socially withdrawn fat kids, though. I was the girl who always wanted to get in the game—even if I played it really, really poorly. I was more than happy to sweat my life away on athletic teams—volleyball, track—if that meant having lots of friends. I was even willing to brave the swim team in a Speedo. I wish I had that kind of body confidence now.

All I remember about playing volleyball and running track as a child is the feeling of constantly trying to keep up with all these kids who were taller and faster than I was, with the sole purpose of earning the right to be in their company, a bona fide member of their club. I couldn't have cared less about winning whatever athletic competition was at stake. All I wanted was to be genuinely accepted by the other members of my team. I was the shortest, I was the slowest, and I was the chubbiest. But I was embraced by my teammates just for playing. That's the great thing about team sports, and the reason I've always encouraged my own boys to play them: trying really hard does count for something. It's hard to be the underdog, but it's even harder to *be against* the underdog.

I gave sports my all even when I wasn't any good at them. I didn't really struggle with a fear of failing whatever athletic task was at hand, because I knew I'd always be able to make everybody laugh, even—or especially—when I came in last. Of course, I was required to play the games according to the same rules as they were, but I was really more of a mascot than an athlete.

Given that I was so active, my teachers and family wondered what was causing my weight problem. Back then, I think I may have been the most puzzled of all.

Looking back on those days now, though, the cause seems very clear: I wanted to vanish, and for good reason.

3

Nothing bad will ever happen to me.

Most seven-year-olds in 1975 were busy cruising around town on their Big Wheels, watching *Wonder Woman*, minding their Pet Rocks and Wombles. Doing the hustle to "Lady Marmalade," cooking up treats in their Easy-Bake Ovens, begging to stay up late enough to watch *Saturday Night Live*.

In most ways, I was the same as every other ordinary seven-year-old in 1975. Except for the way in which I wasn't ordinary at all.

When I was seven, my weight hadn't yet started to inch above my classmates'. I was a curious second grader who wore my caramel cornsilk hair in cheerful pigtails. My closet was filled with crisply ironed Florence Eiseman dresses in a rainbow of bright colors, which were adorned with giant graphic floral appliques that screamed, "Happy kid here!" My personality combined the sweetness of a girly girl, the fearlessness of an adventurous tomboy, and the kindness of an underdog. I was happy-go-lucky and eager to please.

I had no reason to be suspicious of anyone's intentions. I couldn't yet comprehend that a person was capable of saying one thing while doing another. That an intimate touch could feel good but be anything but.

Then I met Joe.

Such a regular, unthreatening name, isn't it? Joe? Even so, even now, almost forty years later and 3,000 miles away, just the sound of that name still has the power to shift my heart into overdrive, to shove my stomach violently up toward my throat.

Life with Joe started out just fine. He was a middle-aged handyman with a slumped-over body and a shriveled-up face. My parents hired him to cheerfully and cheaply complete odd jobs around our house. He replaced light bulbs, did yard work, greased hinges. He specialized in mundane tasks that required no special skills. But because we came to depend on Joe for so many of the little things, he earned our family's trust. By the time he became a threat to me, no one would have suspected a thing.

The big project for which Joe was officially hired was to build a rock wall around our suburban property in Hastings-on-Hudson. My parents thought that such a wall would project an image of strength and containment and keep our family safe. This wall would never be more than symbolic, since it was so low to the ground that even a preschool-age child could climb over it. But even before it was finished, before I realized it would never grow tall enough to hide or shield me, our wall taught me that even the mightiest rocks offer little protection from pain.

Especially when they trap intruders inside instead of out.

During his frequent work breaks, our "handyman" would lead me down to the extra bedroom in our basement.

Our basement, like most other basements in the seventies, was finished. Which meant it had wood paneling and a tired, old daybed.

Over and over again, Joe took me down there and put me on that little bed and touched me. And he made me touch him. And each day, as he built a wall around our house, I tried to build a wall around myself.

It's not as if my parents had left me alone in the house with some strange man. My mother was upstairs the whole time, I'm pretty certain, and I doubt she had any reason to think anything had gone awry. But I've never been able to recall many specific details of what happened. That whole time is fuzzy. And it was fuzzy then in the moment, almost as if it were already a memory at the same time it was happening.

This seemed to go on for months. When he looked down at me, heavy with desire, he resembled a raisin wearing a gray wool cap.

One thing I do know is that the vague sense of my mother's presence in the house while Joe was abusing me made me somehow feel that what was being done to me was okay with her. Now, as a parent, I shudder at how easy it is for a determined predator to seize its prey and for a child to misunderstand her parent's reaction, or lack thereof.

As the rock wall he was hired to build grew to surround our home, I felt as though I were shrinking. I was living in a constant state of confusion. What was the point of building a wall if it offered no protection? What was the point of having a mother if she offered you no mothering?

Afternoons with Joe became part of my new normal. Those days mark my first memories of feeling deeply conflicted. On one hand, what was happening filled me with an ominous sense of unease; it made me want to exist outside myself. On the other hand, there was no denying that there were moments when what Joe was doing to me seemed to feel—in a purely sensory way—pretty good. The places where he was touching me had been designed for pleasure, after all.

This collusion of right and wrong confused me for decades. Your body was not designed to feel bad about something that makes you feel good. Being violated by Joe, so unsure how I felt about it, gave me the sense that my body was more likely to betray than support me.

I began to doubt my own perceptions and judgments of the world at large—not just the world in that downstairs bedroom. I shut down completely.

⟶⟵

I can't remember what finally led to my telling my parents about the abuse. I can't remember where we were or what I said. By the time I told them what Joe had done to me, the lasting damage had been done. I had become closed off.

I watched my parents confront Joe. I was hiding below the window line in our living room, which faced our front yard. I kneeled on the wall-to-wall carpeted floor, propping myself up by the elbows on a chrome bench upholstered in velour. My eye level was just high enough to see out the picture window. Safe and invisible, I watched the fierce pantomime of my parents reprimanding the wizened old man for what he'd done to me.

Seeing the scene unfold, I was terrified and humiliated—and I somehow felt guilty, whether for telling on him and getting him in trouble, or for deriving some release of pleasure from watching him be punished.

After Joe was let go that day, I remember waiting for relief to set in. The villain had been banished to the other side of the wall. I was safe now.

But that feeling of relief never came, probably because no one in my family spoke of Joe or what he had done to me ever again.

I contained myself on the outside, but inside I was deeply terrified and humiliated. My parents were tense. My sister was clueless. And although the man was gone, the feelings were not.

The fact that my parents refused to address what had happened to me filled me with shame and self-doubt. Was it possible that nothing had really happened to me? Had I gotten Joe punished for nothing?

In 1983, when I was fourteen years old, a child abuse scandal rocked the nation and dominated the airwaves. Called "The McMartin Preschool Trial," the case brought sexual abuse charges against numerous members of one family who ran a day care center in California.

Each night, as we had done ever since I could remember, my family watched television together in my parents' bedroom before we went to sleep. That year, no matter what we were watching, breaking news updates on "McMartin," as it came to be called, interrupted programming. It had been seven years since I'd watched my parents banish Joe from our home, but my cheeks lit on fire whenever a newscaster uttered the words *child abuse*. I worried that everyone was looking at me. As I sat in front of my family, facing the television, I could feel their eyes on my neck. I stared straight through the screen, scrunching my body up against the foot of my parents' bed.

I prayed no one would say anything about it. I was still humiliated by what had happened, ashamed of what I had been through. Nobody had explained to me that it hadn't been my fault. Nobody had told me that sometimes confused people do terrible things to children and that it takes a long time to recover from such a trauma. Nobody told me how sorry they were.

I suppose everyone just assumed that I had forgotten about it—pushed it out of my mind. I took for granted that the constant updates on McMartin would force my parents to remember the horrible things that had been done to me: *This terrible brand of abuse has touched someone in our very own family! How strong she is! Let's shower her with healing love.* I realize now, though, that it's possible my parents didn't associate McMartin with me at all. Everyone else had moved on, and since I never spoke about it, they probably assumed that I had too.

And why hadn't I forgotten about it, I asked my childhood, then teenage, self over and over and over again? What was wrong with me? Why did I think about it every time I saw my naked body in the mirror? Why had I grown to hate my body so much?

Because it's your body that made him do it to you in the first place, said a terrible, inhuman voice somewhere deep inside. *It's your body's fault.*

Because of the pain Joe had caused me, I never wanted anyone to look at my stupid body ever again. I would have to figure out a way to make myself invisible.

Like so many other survivors of childhood sexual abuse, I did this by eating. I smuggled forbidden candy upstairs to my room in the middle of the night by hiding it in the folds of my nightgown. I heated myself up a second Hungry Man dinner even after my stomach was already churning over with the salty, gooey warmth of the first.

Nothing made me feel better than gorging myself. It had both long-term and short-term results. Not only did overeating result in hiding my emerging feminine shape, but it also bathed my body in the numbness of addiction. And of course it kept me quiet: I knew it wasn't polite to talk with my mouth full.

To this day, I believe that it was my parents' silence in the wake of the abuse—even more than the abuse itself—that wounded me so badly. What could be more destructive than never speaking of a trauma that teaches a little girl to treat her own body like an enemy? Because my parents never helped me to make sense of what happened, my inexperienced, unsophisticated child's mind contorted the meaning of what had transpired into something I'd brought on myself.

The longer I kept what Joe had done to me a secret, the more weight I put on. The weight not only insulated me from the attention of other men, but it also made it easier to stay quiet, somehow. My pain was deep down inside me, but I kept building a facade on top of it.

The McMartin trial stretched on for what seemed like forever. After years and years of investigations and arrests and hearings, nobody was ever convicted, and all charges were dropped. Nobody ever really knew what happened. Everyone accused was acquitted. It ended up being the most expensive criminal trial in US history.

4

*"You'll never get anywhere if
you don't lose weight."*

As I inched my way toward puberty—more like "footed" my way, considering the exponential extent to which my girth seemed to be growing—my mother became openly concerned about my weight. By the time I was ten or eleven years old and fatter than ever, it was clear this wasn't baby fat, but a preview of the adult fat that was yet to come. And having a fat daughter was one problem my mother wasn't going to be silent about.

Before she expressed her dissatisfaction in words, it came through loud and clear in the bitter way she looked at me each time I reached for a cookie or a second helping. She was trying to communicate with me in a secret mother-daughter language, I guess—*Stop now. Don't make me say it out loud and embarrass you*—but her punishing glances failed to squelch my hunger.

Ironically she was offering me my first taste of delicious rebellion. Her admonishments just made me want to eat more, so I did. Sometimes to spite her, I stuffed my face.

Finally, my mother opened her own pinched mouth, seething—*Do you really think you need that, Ricki?*—in the hopes that I'd learn to shut mine. When, after seeing *Annie* on Broadway, I told my mother that I wanted desperately to audition, she quickly squashed my hopes, rolling her eyes and saying, "You're not exactly the starving orphan type."

Finally living up to cultural stereotypes—my weight problem had helped her get in touch with her long-dormant maternal instincts—she tried to help me slim down, to no avail. Well, when I say "tried to help me slim down," what I really mean is that my mother criticized me every way she could. *Why did I look so different from my friends?* she asked. *Why couldn't I just learn to control myself? What made me think I was so special, that I didn't need to worry about my weight?*

Little did I know, my mother was grappling with her own body-image issues. She bragged about having gained just eleven pounds while she was pregnant with me, dieting and smoking throughout the pregnancy.

Far from motivating me to change my body, my mother's criticism galvanized my identity as "overweight-and-okay-with-it" or, rather, "overweight-and-not-giving-a-shit-how-much-it-might-piss-off-my-mother." I gained weight to spite her. Looking back now, I see that maintaining my heft was a silent form of rebellion, an ingenious way to simultaneously assert my individuality and disappear.

But thanks to the strength of my spirit, or perhaps some divine intervention on the part of Grandma Sylvia, being overweight didn't stop me from playing sports or winning a spot in a prestigious children's theater troupe in New York City. It didn't stop me from fantasizing about being an actress.

In fact, it didn't even stop me from taking concrete steps toward living the life of a professional one.

Ever since seeing *Annie* on Broadway, I had been determined to be a performer.

My first gig as a paid entertainer consisted of singing and dancing as a company member of a kids' cabaret in New York City when I was about fourteen years old. Picture a sort of low-rent *Mickey Mouse Club*, with kids wearing T-shirts emblazoned with their names spelled out in balloon letters. I went to school in Westchester all week, then performed in Manhattan every weekend. My first exposure to the cabaret had been as an audience member, and from the moment the curtains opened, I knew I had to be a part of its club one day. (Unlike my desire to be in *Annie*, joining this motley crew, with their budget costumes and varying levels of physical beauty, was a goal that seemed reachable.)

In seventh grade, I auditioned for the cabaret and was immediately offered a spot in the company. I was overwhelmed with joy and anticipation of my new life among people who would understand me. The troupe's director was a homely, gray-haired lady named Toukie Weinstein, who had started her career as a talent agent and evolved into this Miss Hanniganesque figure who presided over a ragtag group of talented New York City kids ranging in age from middle to high school.

Although she was the one who offered me entrance to the group, Toukie was emotionally abusive to me from the start. She had cast me, it seemed, to serve as her portable punching bag. Toukie would pick on me for no reason, making cracks about my weight or my timing being off (when it wasn't). I just smiled and swallowed all the undeserved criticism Toukie dished out, never talking back or acting out. Because she too had weight issues, I wonder now if perhaps Toukie was expressing her anger toward herself by beating up on me. I wish I'd considered that possibility at the time. Maybe then I wouldn't have felt so ashamed of myself.

Because the way Toukie treated me always put me on the defensive, I didn't develop close relationships with any of the other kids in the cabaret with the exception of the one other fat girl, whom Toukie also beat up. Our fatness was pretty much the only thing we had in common, so our friendship didn't end up being a lifelong one. I see now that one didn't exactly need a PhD to figure out how Toukie's own self-esteem issues affected her teaching style. If only I had been able to see the whole picture back then, when I was taking out my teacher's issues on myself.

Despite the fact that being part of the cabaret meant my having to endure Toukie's harsh words, I look back on participating in it as one of the formative experiences in creating my identity, style, and work ethic as a performer.

As I sang my number, a torchy, 1960s beach movie song called "Where the Boys Are," which positively frothed with adolescent longing, I learned how to relate to an audience: How to make eye contact and when to look off into the distance. When to pull back into my softest, most intimate voice and when to belt it out. When to smile and when to milk the sadness pooling in my puppy-dog eyes for all it was worth.

As a performer in the cabaret, I was good enough that when some producers decided to make a low-budget movie featuring a select group of kids from the troupe, they asked me if I wanted to be in it.

"OF COURSE!" was my reply. "BE IN A MOVIE?" This was my dream!

All I had to do to make my dream a reality was to meet with one of the producers of the film, whose name was Mario, so he could make sure I was right for the part.

Piece of cake, I thought. Even then I knew I gave a good interview. I wasn't nervous about securing my role.

But my mother was, and she didn't want me to rest on my laurels. "This is by no means a sure thing, Ricki," she said, in a grave, intense voice. "You be nice to him."

Looking back on that moment now, I wonder, *What did my mother mean?* She knew what kind of kid I was—that I was innocent and green and eager to please. What did she expect me to do if she hadn't bothered to remind me to be nice? Spit in his eye? What exactly did she mean by "be nice," anyway?

When the day came for me to lobby for my role, I went to the movie producer's apartment. He lived in a famous building downtown. This neighborhood seemed exotic and cosmopolitan to my suburban self, yet when I first set eyes on it, I felt oddly at home.

I took the elevator up to Mario's floor and found the door

to his apartment. After I entered his place, which was decorated with that special panache found only in the very early eighties, with brightly colored furniture and geometric light fixtures, Mario invited me to sit next to him on the sofa, asking whether I might like to watch some TV together.

"Sure," I said, thinking maybe it was a little bit unusual to watch TV during an audition, but who was I to complain? I loved television, after all, and sitting silently on the sofa would certainly be easier than performing my monologue. I wanted to go with the flow. I remembered what my mother had told me: *Be nice to him.* Maybe this was what she meant.

As I sank back into the quicksand couch, my feet dangling what seemed like miles above the shaggy carpet, Mario sidled up very close to me and used a giant prehistoric remote controller to play a videotape he'd cued up before my arrival.

I stared at the screen in anticipation, wondering what we'd watch. Some excellent child monologues to inspire my performance? Young Liza Minnelli belting out a ballad to prove that a child really could sound like a woman? A Bob Fosse dance routine to give me a sense of the edgy direction the choreographer wanted to go in?

None of the above. This video had nothing to do with my training as an actress or my role in the film. This video depicted a man and woman so close together that it was hard to distinguish whose limbs were whose. This couple was going at it. There was no talking, just low music. I'd never seen anything like it, but it made me feel wildly uncomfortable. Especially as I looked over at Mario who was smiling oddly and desperately trying to make eye contact with me.

Totally flustered, I remained paralyzed on that sofa. This

was so confusing. I knew that Mario wasn't really doing anything to me. But I felt just as awful—as mystified, as powerless—as I had years before when Joe had touched me in the basement. What was this mysterious power older men seemed to have? I felt a surge of stress hormones. My body knew something was wrong, even if my head couldn't identify what.

Although I kept looking in the general direction of the video in order to please Mario, my eyes and mind kept it out of focus. I just stared straight ahead, as Mario's body, next to me, radiated an electricity I could tell he wanted me to pick up on. I avoided interacting with him entirely.

Eventually the video was over, and Mario was smiling widely. He didn't ask me to sing or dance or recite anything. In fact, I'd almost forgotten what I had gone to Mario's house to do in the first place. He thanked me and told me I was free to go. I bolted out the door, skipping the elevator; instead, practically gliding down the stairs to the lobby, whooshing through the swinging glass door, and running away from the building. For the first time in my life, I was eager to get back to the suburbs.

Later that evening, my mother wanted a full report. "How did it go?" she asked anxiously. She actually seemed to care. This was one of the odd days when she appeared to be rooting for me.

I was unsure how to answer her. It almost didn't feel that what had happened up in Mario's apartment could have been real. Since Mario hadn't really made me do anything, I thought I might be overreacting to the sense of uneasiness I felt. Still, I knew our meeting hadn't exactly been kosher. I had the distinct feeling I might have done something wrong, but I genuinely didn't know what it was. I had been trying so desperately to do everything right.

"It was a little bit weird," I told my mother finally.

"What do you mean?" she asked, her face and voice utterly devoid of compassion, more exasperated than anything else. Any sense of excitement for me, of anticipation of good things in my future, was gone. She looked as though my sheer existence were a total nuisance to her. To her defense, she had no idea what had happened up in Mario's apartment.

"Um, he made me, you know—kinda uncomfortable. We watched a really—adult—movie." I took a deep breath, trying to decide whether I could trust my mother with the fear that I'd just felt. Maybe she'd be kind. Maybe she'd understand. "I was afraid he was going to try something."

My mother laughed, even snorted a little, as if to say, *Aren't you a stupid little baby?* Then, looking down at my belly, she said, "Don't be ridiculous, Ricki. He's a movie producer. He couldn't possibly be attracted to someone as fat as you."

Even now I feel the sting. The embarrassment. The confusion. The shame. The repression. The desire to make everything okay again. Why did she think I wanted him to be attracted to me? How had she managed to so invert the situation that I now was worried about not being pretty enough to attract a child molester?

Many years later, relatively thin and undeniably successful, I was looking to buy a place in downtown New York. My Realtor told me about a once-in-a-lifetime listing: Britney Spears's knockout penthouse in the same well-known apartment building. I rushed down to look at it.

I'm not sure whether I recognized the address right away,

but I started to feel a wave of nausea as we approached the building, and the moment I stepped into the lobby, all the pain of that "audition" came rushing back. I couldn't stand to be there for even a second.

Who cares whether you've arrived, when you're not the one choosing your destination?

5

No one will ever believe in me.

⌐⌐⌐

When you're just a kid, you don't understand that nine times out of ten when grown-ups say something cruel to you, they're usually just expressing a problem they have with themselves. I'm not sure when I realized that my mother's harsh criticism of me most likely stemmed from her own deep self-loathing, but this epiphany offered cold comfort from the icy freezer burn she emitted in place of cozy, maternal love.

Even in my early teen years, I reached back in time for warm memories of Grandma Sylvia, who had managed to make me feel like a worthwhile human being. Like a star, even.

Despite Toukie's constant criticism and Mario's highly inappropriate behavior, I worked hard as a cast member of the children's cabaret and movie. I stayed out of trouble and concentrated on improving as a performer. I was propelled by a strong sense of purpose: to prove my naysayers wrong. I had nobody to rely on but myself, and although this was a painful truth to come to terms with at such a young age, it was excellent training for my chosen career path.

Although Toukie moonlighted as a personal talent manager who worked tirelessly trying to turn many of the kids in the group into big stars, she never once asked if she could represent me. I suppose she didn't see me as talented enough to bother managing—or maybe she saw me as too fat to waste her time on. Either way, her discouragement served as a powerful motivator for me to succeed.

Toukie certainly wasn't the only authority figure to discourage me in the years before my career took off, but she might have been the most important. Why? Toukie showed me, in the simplest of terms, that grown-ups can be wrong.

My whole thing growing up was that I wanted to be liked by everyone. I always tried to be popular, to be looked up to. As a child who was so eager to please but who received so little feedback, that was my shtick. *Just you wait, haters. I'll win you over.*

Ten years later, even after I had developed career confidence from my movie appearances and having my own talk show, I remained the underdog everybody was rooting for rather than the sure thing. I don't want that charm to ever go away. I guess I should thank the naysayers for giving me the secret of my success.

6

I'll never stand out among the talented kids.

～⌒～

Like most other theater-obsessed kids in the 1980s, I was glued
to the television whenever *Fame* was on. What could be dreamier
than an entire high school full of singing and dancing kids like
me? The moment I realized "the Fame school" was real, I knew
I wanted to go there. While I didn't go to the real "Fame" school—
a public school called La Guardia, a.k.a. "Music and Art"—I did
attend a school that valued performance over academics, even
though its founders intended it to do just the opposite.

New York City's Professional Children's School (PCS) was
established in 1914 under the mission of providing the city's
young vaudevillians with an education. When it was founded,
PCS was a powerful institution passionate about child advocacy.
By the time I got there, though, it was less a political hotbed and
more a diploma mill.

In the eighties, **PCS** could have basically been called "Broadway Prep." I practiced my math and reading comprehension in the company of such schoolmates as the Cosby kids, Jane Krakowski, Martha Plimpton, and a host of willowy dancers from the school at Lincoln Center's American Ballet Theater. Looking back, it's sort of ridiculous that I was allowed to matriculate to PCS. I was neither working professionally on a show or film nor studying music or dance seriously. PCS was an excuse for me to avoid having to endure the pain of a real academic education, since the schoolwork was notoriously easy and you could skip class pretty much whenever you wanted as long as you had a "good reason." Lest you think my admission to the institution was somehow an indication of my talent or star quality, let me assure you that entrance requirements were fairly straightforward: anyone who could convince their parents to pay $6,000 a year for a mediocre education was allowed in.

Why did my parents let me go? I think, despite feeling dubious about my chances of success in the performance world, they were keen to throw our hats in the ring. And while it's true that my mother never really had any faith in me, I think my father did. A little bit of his own mother—Grandma Sylvia—still glowed inside him. (Many years later, as an adult, I found out that my Grandma Sylvia had never been particularly fond of my mother. I always knew I took after her.)

By the time I was a senior at **PCS**, I weighed well over 200 pounds. Looking back, I marvel at the fact that I had the confidence to persevere in becoming a performer, despite having to shoulder such an obvious aesthetic disadvantage as compared to my peers. Translation: I knew the world thought the skinny kids in my class were hot, I knew the world thought I, pleasantly plump, was not, and still, I kept on dancing for my life.

My favorite part of the "school day" at PCS came when the bell rang and I headed downtown to Grand Central Station to catch the commuter train home. I knew that waiting there at Grand Central for me, without fail, would be two of my closest friends: Hot Dog Number One and Hot Dog Number Two. They were always ready and waiting for me to pick them up on my way home. We had the best time on the train ride home together! I beefed up so we'd have even more in common.

Strangely enough, in a not entirely negative way, my weight distinguished me from the pack of talented kids I went to school with. Even though my size called a sometimes unwelcome sort of attention to me, it called attention nonetheless. And you know what they say: in show business, there's no such thing as bad publicity.

More than with the Broadway and TV stars, I hung out with the school's offbeat film actors, who shared my rebellious spirit. (By "rebellious spirit," I mean I didn't spend all day practicing pirouettes or scales, but rather sneaking into movies and mainlining popcorn.) I was so unconventional, I went to prom with a couple: My schoolmate Martha Plimpton and her boyfriend River Phoenix. At the time, they were riding high on the success of their film *Running on Empty*. They were also madly in love, so on a "date" with them on what was supposed to be one of the most important nights of my high school social career, I felt less like a teenage girl than I did a chaperone. The best part of my prom night was the Indian restaurant that River, Martha, my date, and I ended up in. It was called Nirvana, and the night wasn't a total loss because the naan bread they served there brought me pretty close to that state.

When I was a teenager, my self-image was, in a word, fractured. On the one hand, I felt like the most appealing and entertaining person in the world (God bless you, Grandma Sylvia). On the other, I knew I was disgustingly fat and totally undesirable (thanks, Mom and Toukie). But wait—actually, I suppose I wasn't really undesirable at all? (Joe and Mario had taught me that lesson.) It was all so confusing. Since my vision of myself was based entirely on the opinions of others, and those opinions varied wildly depending on context, I suppose my feelings of brokenness made perfect sense.

Walking around Manhattan all alone, most girls on the verge of womanhood have to contend with an onslaught of catcalls from construction workers perched on the scaffolding high above the sidewalk. We've all heard the complex emotions solicited by these groups of lascivious men described countless times: *They were salivating like wild animals. I felt like a piece of meat. I was terrified by how much they wanted me.*

But my own story was different. As a hormone-propelled teenage girl passing a group of construction workers, all I heard were moos and a slew of painfully insulting nicknames. The only feedback I got from the opposite sex was that I was totally undesirable.

While part of me would have loved a whistle or two, given that my only sexual experience had transpired with a perverted handyman and a "movie producer," failing to pique the interest of a group of uncouth men on the street was just fine with me.

And although I was lonely, there was an unexpected benefit to my not having to worry about negotiating the world of dating: it enabled me to keep my focus sharp on becoming a star. I knew that was the only way I could be truly happy.

7

*I'll never get discovered, stuck out
in the middle of nowhere.*

When I graduated from the Professional Children's School, stardom didn't seem to be in the cards for me. I wasn't about to skip college without a solid excuse, and since I hadn't landed any plum roles as a 200-pound eighteen-year-old barely out of high school, getting back on a "normal" life path seemed to be my only option: Ithaca College, the only school I got into. To put it mildly, I wasn't really dying to go there. Ithaca College was located 230 miles away from Manhattan, the center of my universe, in the suicide capital of upstate New York (or America, for that matter—look it up).

Sitting down with my parents to discuss my college choices of Ithaca, Ithaca, and Ithaca, I threw up my hands and said, "It's settled, then! I'll just move to Manhattan, and go on auditions, and work in a restaurant or something until I hit it big. Obviously you don't expect me to move to Antarctica."

My father sat back in his chair, a pained look on his face. While he wasn't exactly my champion, he didn't like to see me disappointed. My mother, however, made her perspective crystal clear: "Ithaca has an excellent musical theater department. Whether it's a good idea for you to continue on with musical theater or not, I won't bother to discuss." Her voice trailed off in a sigh. "With your grades, and your—" (She cut herself off for a minute, but I swear she was going to say, "your weight.") "If you ask me," she continued, "you're lucky to get in." My father looked at me sympathetically but didn't offer any opinion. Where was Grandma Sylvia when I needed her? It appeared my fate was sealed. I was about to board a one-way train to mediocrity.

Ithaca College was, in a word, depressing. I figured out pretty soon after arriving there that the drama department, however well regarded, was not likely to catapult me to stardom. This message came to me loud and clear from my academic advisor, a voice and movement teacher named Fern Platt. Ms. Platt was only an assistant professor, but she acted as if she were the college president. She made it her business to look students up and down with a smug, critical look on her face, conveying clearly that never was she happier than when standing in judgment.

I had actually arrived on campus with a good attitude, thinking, *At least I'll be able to perform lots of different kinds of roles, get my feet wet. Everyone will be impressed by me! I've already performed professionally! Maybe I'll even be able to mentor students with less experience. It'll be nice to be valued for my talent for a change.*

That was before I met Ms. Platt. With her stringy red hair, mousy face, and lumpy body, she was anything but physically intimidating. But she was a bully. From the moment she got a good long look at me, she took it upon herself to break some bad news. She told me in a hushed, condescending voice that I simply was not talented, and my dream of a career in the performing arts was something I should give up.

"The sooner you accept that it's unlikely for you to make it, the better," she said. "It will hurt so much less that way."

Nice advice, right? Perhaps she was speaking from personal experience, though I never found out for sure. I was pretty bummed for a day or two, but then I gathered up my naysayer kryptonite and decided not to listen to Ms. Platt. What did that bitch know anyway, stuck teaching at some institution upstate? It wasn't like *her* name was lighting up Broadway marquees, for God's sake. ("PRESENTING FERN PLATT?" I don't think so.)

There's so much truth to the cliché, "Those who can't do, teach." Those who have been forced to give up their own career aspirations to help students achieve theirs may be harboring some serious resentment. Teachers can blow a toxic cloud of envy at their students when they feel their own career has been a disappointment, sometimes even appearing to take pleasure in making those with promise feel small. By this point, though, I had plenty of experience at being undervalued and discouraged by authority figures, so I knew they weren't always right.

Right or not, Fern Platt succeeded in keeping me out of the Ithaca College limelight. Despite singing and dancing my heart out at auditions, I didn't get cast in one show. Ms. Platt gave me a C in voice and movement, which was horrible given that it was my major, and I knew I could attribute this disappointing grade to the fact that I was fat, not because I couldn't sing and dance. (Okay, maybe it was also a teeny-weeny bit due to the fact that my voice and movement class took place at 8:00 AM, and, as I told *People* magazine once, "I can't open my eyes at 8 in the morning, let alone grunt like a pig.")

Despite trying desperately to keep my chin—okay, chins—up, I was feeling defeated both socially and academically. I tried to switch departments to pursue a communications major. If all else failed, at least I'd always be able to communicate somehow. But the professors in charge refused to transfer my credits. They said that in order to choose a new academic path, I would have to start college all over again. The prospect of an additional day in Ithaca, much less an additional semester, filled me with dread.

I ventured into my very first college finals week feeling as though I were carrying a backpack filled with lead. I vowed to tell my parents that I was leaving Ithaca to go back to auditioning full time, no matter what they thought. I wasn't going to waste my life being made to feel like shit by people who felt like shit about themselves.

And then I heard the words that would change my life forever: "Director John Waters is seeking a fat girl who can really dance."

He was making a movie called *Hairspray*.

Those words were all I needed to hear in order to get the hell out of Ithaca. "There aren't that many roles you're right for," said a voice inside my head, at once wise and cruel, "so just go ahead and read for them. Who knows when you'll get another chance to audition for a part worth taking?"

"You said I wasn't good? Fuck you!" sang the voice inside my head to Fern Platt. "I'll show you, Platt! I'm gonna make it! Big!"

I threw my stuff into garbage bags and shoved them all into my car. Soon I'd be in New York City. A five-hour, all-night drive wouldn't deter me from rushing out to meet a fringe film director. This was my shot, and I was going to take it. I wanted desperately to break free of my boring collegiate life and become the star Grandma Sylvia always told me I would be. I'd been waiting for this day ever since the first time I heard Annie sing "Tomorrow," and now tomorrow was finally here.

At the time I decided to make the pilgrimage to that audition, I didn't even know who John Waters was. It was a rarefied group who had seen *Pink Flamingos,* and to be honest, many of them lived in San Francisco, performing in drag cabarets. But I salivated at the thought of being cast as the world's only fat ingenue—with rhythm, no less!—and I didn't care which niche counterculture decided to embrace me as long as one of them did.

I felt a huge sense of relief at the fact that at this audition, my being overweight would be regarded as a positive thing instead of a check mark against me. Excess weight was key to this character, Tracy, who was described as "a big girl who moves like a skinny one." I even wore baggy clothes to the audition in order to make myself look as large as possible. I wanted my moves to seem delicate, feminine, and agile in comparison to my size.

The first audition took place in the tiny office of John Waters's casting director, Mary Calhoun, a teeny-tiny round woman who looked more like a school lunch lady than the woman who held the keys to my future. As I sat across the desk from John, wearing a huge ITHACA COLLEGE sweatshirt, I could see him straining forward in his chair, trying to ascertain how big I actually was underneath all that fleece.

As John leaned in to study my form, I felt like a Macy's Thanksgiving parade float being ogled by a toddler. This was not an unfamiliar feeling, of course. Every actor knows that a director wants to know what he or she is buying and is entitled to gawk. I was used to sucking in, stretching upward, elongating my neck, drawing in my rib cage: feeling painfully self-conscious about being too fat for a part. But this time, the concern was whether I was fat enough. (Hallelujah! Thank God for the gays! Having my appeal assessed by a homosexual male was something I'd both celebrate and suffer through many more times, throughout both my work and personal life in the years to come.)

Self-conscious about how fat I looked, even though I was supposed to look as fat as possible, I followed the fat girl's rules to live by: *When in doubt, make them laugh. Insult yourself before they have a chance to insult you.* "It's all me," I croaked gleefully, gesturing to the curves and rolls that defined my body. John's gaze fixed on my lumpy bits, which were barely concealed by yards and yards of sweatshirt material. "I promise, I'm just as fat as I look!" Cue trademark giggle. I had never before uttered such a liberating sentence.

John must have liked what he saw because he invited me on the spot to return for a callback. I was nervous and excited, but it felt right. John had given me back the swagger Fern Platt had tried to snatch away.

⸻

The callback was in a more official-seeming rehearsal room than the tiny office where the audition had been held. This time, we needed space because we had to dance. A bunch of chairs were set up outside the rehearsal room for all the prospective Tracys to wait in, and I sat down next to a rotund girl who was a dead ringer for the old comic book character Little Lotta. Weighing at least 300 pounds, she wore a Peter Pan collar and a huge, cheerful bow in her hair. Just the sight of her filled me with intimidation. No one could have looked more the part.

I decided to strike up a conversation. Long ago, I'd learned how important it was to win over my enemies. "You're really pretty," I said to Little Lotta, in a vaguely pathetic voice that must have projected my sense of imminent defeat.

"Shlank hyoo," she replied.

Holy speech impediment, Batman! Taken by surprise, I turned my reflexive laugh into a pretend cough. YES! Little Lotta's speaking issue could be described only as a gift from the divine, providing the extra burst of confidence I needed to nail that callback audition.

I came, I danced, I triumphed. I could do the mashed potato, the twist. And Mr. Waters and his associate, Baltimore legend Pat Moran, sure did seem to like it like this! Not to mention that nobody needed convincing when it came to the extent of my pulchritude: when I let loose, my jiggly bits wiggled like crazy.

Although I didn't think my dancing was *all that*—I had quit studying tap and ballet when I was really little because everybody knows fat girls shouldn't focus on *movement*—my charm was all in my attitude. Out of all the big girls lined up in the hallway, spilling all over their aluminum folding chairs, I was the one who was the least uncomfortable with my body. I appeared to be having fun in real life, not just acting like it.

John Waters gave me the job on the spot.

For most girls, the idea of a fairy godmother was sheer fantasy, but I had been sent a real one. From the moment we started working together, John and I shared a real sense of gratitude for each other. Our relationship has always been symbiotic in the truest sense of the word. I wouldn't even have a career if it weren't for John, and his career took a totally new path after he met me.

So just over a year after graduating from the Professional Children's School, nine months after bailing from Ithaca College, I made my starring film debut in John Waters's *Hairspray*. I was still weighing in at an impressive 200 pounds, but suddenly I had become the girl who gets the guy, wins the dance contest, and becomes a star. This was confusing, to say the least—but finally it was confusing in a good way. Was it possible that the negative things my mother had been telling me all these years weren't true after all? Had all my naysayers been wrong? Was it possible that what Joe had done hadn't ruined me forever? Maybe that disgusting letch Mario really *had* thought I was pretty?

I didn't worry about answering all these questions. The real triumph was that I was suddenly asking them. I am so grateful for my own resiliency—that I was able to hold on to any sense of self-esteem for so long despite receiving virtually no positive reinforcement.

What would have happened had John Waters never invented Tracy Turnblad? I don't know. But I do know that to me, she was nothing short of a gift. Playing Tracy enabled me to take what most people see as a handicap, my weight, and turn it into an asset.

That I was able to build a career on my greatest "flaw" is at least in part credit to a strong sense of self-worth buried deep inside me. Working on *Hairspray* was no cakewalk. Of course I was self-conscious about my body in certain situations, particularly when I was interacting with boys, but when it was time to perform, I truly believed that I deserved that leading role, and that confidence came through in my performance.

Plain and simple, I knew that I had the best personality, that I was the best dancer, and that I deserved the heart of the gorgeous guy.

Even though she was in my life for only a very short time, I attribute this strong faith in myself to Grandma Sylvia.

And, of course, an overwhelming desire to get the hell out of Hastings-on-Hudson and into Hollywood.

8

I'll never be a sex object.

⸻

In the fantastical universe of John Waters, being different doesn't necessarily mean you're not sexually attractive. In John's hometown of Baltimore, Maryland, land of the soft crab and the chicken box, "unconventional" equals "in demand." John Waters is a man who sees the beauty in everyone, from drag queens to beauty queens, plain Janes to janitors. When you're looking at the world through John's lens, it's what's different about you that makes you amazing, not how successful you are in your quest to look like everybody else.

On the set of *Hairspray*, I experienced nothing short of bliss in finally being given permission to embrace my sensual side in spite of my weight. I had never felt entitled to really feel desire for another human being, simply because I assumed I deserved to be punished because of my size. Find me a fat girl who feels entitled to much of anything. Society's constant admonishments teach her to restrict, restrict, restrict; to manage her impulses. Nobody ever gave me permission to want.

Until I became Tracy Turnblad, I felt almost foolish imagining anyone could ever want me *that* way. In Baltimore, though, I felt the freedom to enjoy being a girl. I danced dirtily. I wantonly displayed my animal yearnings just as openly as had the catcallers who used to torment me on New York streets. I developed the true self-confidence that comes with actually believing, not just repeating, that I had something special to offer the world.

In what many people have told me is their favorite scene in *Hairspray,* my character is in jail after being arrested for protesting segregation and taking part in race riots. Watching television with my cell mates, I notice the image of my teen heartthrob boyfriend Link Larkin (played by Elvis Presley look-alike Michael St. Gerard) pop-up on screen. When Link's gorgeous image takes shape on that 1960s TV screen, my character, Tracy, refuses to censor her yearnings. I stick out my pubescent tongue, run up to the television, and shamelessly lick Link's image like a hungry cat. Although the screen tasted more like Windex than young love, that lick marked a real moment of transformation for me—I was finally unafraid to exhibit my desire publicly.

John Waters taught me how to want things. I always did my best acting with him because he was clear and direct: he gave me line readings, showing me a glimpse of the person he wanted me to be in the film, a person I could be in real life. He broadened my own vision of what I could be. The movie came out in February 1988, ten years to the day after my Grandma Sylvia's death, and I smiled thinking about how proud she would be of me.

When you see my character relating to Michael's character in the film, whether we're dancing with each other across the room in the "Negro" record shop or making out with each other sloppily, like all the other kids, there's a confidence in my eyes that had never been there before. This was the freedom John gave me.

Because he wanted our chemistry to be real and the experience to be fun, John even let me select one of my love interests—the boy that my character, Tracy Turnblad, would partner with at "ladies' choice," and whom she would kiss on screen. Considering I hadn't had too much experience making out in real life, I was very much looking forward to my first PDA. This extremely cute extra, whom I had ordered as though he were a pizza, seemed to like me too.

Being cast as an object of desire on the set of *Hairspray*, I began to pack away the pain caused by the mooing construction workers tormenting me on my way to school, the sting of my mother's admonishing eye, the critical voice of my childhood acting coach muttering that my career wasn't likely to go anywhere. I began to believe in the power of my own attractiveness despite my being different from the norm. I started to understand the compliments I had long been given by others, which I had always brushed off as false praise, appreciating the twinkle in my eyes, the curve of my back, the curl of my upper lip. I grew more and more excited as the shoot date for my on-screen kiss neared.

But just before we were supposed to shoot that sweet teenage moment, a bitter taste flooded my mouth, reminding me of my old life as an undesirable nobody: I found out that my kissing partner had been making fun of me behind my back, cracking fat jokes to the other actors and crew members. Seems he'd been flirting with me just to secure his place in the scene, but his true feelings for me were as negative as the insecure part of me feared they were. What a phony.

I was devastated by this betrayal, since I'd been made a fool of in front of a group of people whose opinions I really cared about. The set of a John Waters film is very much like summer camp: everyone knows everyone else, and everybody gossips nonstop. I was sure I could hear the whispers everywhere I went—nowhere louder, though, than in my own head.

How could you have thought for even one minute that someone like that *could like someone like* you? hissed an ugly voice deep inside me.

I couldn't believe nobody had told me the truth about this heartless jerk. Did they really think that I was so pathetic, I didn't even deserve to know what was being said behind my back? All these people whom I had considered to be my friends let me look like a fool for God knows how long.

But who could blame him for not wanting me?

Who was I kidding, believing I had something to offer?

I was huge and unattractive, and I wouldn't want me either.

<hr>

One of the best parts about doing *Hairspray* was getting to know the incredible performer who played my mother in the movie, whom *People* magazine called "the drag queen of the century."

Divine had been working with John since the beginning of each of their careers. In the 1960s, they had a theater troupe called the Dreamlanders. It was John who had given the man who was born Harris Glenn Milstead his fabulous stage name.

I was in awe of Divine. He had such an amazing life story, and everybody on set delighted in sharing details of his biography. *Did you know Divine went to beauty school? He can do a perfect beehive! Did you know Divine was raised a Baptist? He grew up rich, did you know that? His real name is Glenn! Did you know he was once the prime suspect in a grisly murder? He's had more than one number-one disco hit! Did you know he ate real dog poop in* Pink Flamingos? *Real dog poop!*

Just being around the ever fearless Divine made me feel safe, protected, and optimistic. I'm not sure why, but I think his presence affected me on a couple of levels. One was that he was a shining example of how happy a person could become by being 100 percent true to himself. *Nobody* told Divine what to do. He was a true original.

Second, he felt uncannily like a parallel-universe parent to me. All the warmth and intensity my own parents lacked, Divine radiated. I felt instantly connected to him, even though he didn't really like me at first. He must have felt that I was infringing on his territory, since he had played both the mother and the daughter in all of John Waters's other movies, and he probably felt he still deserved both roles. But *Hairspray* represented John's chance to move into the mainstream, and casting me, a biological girl who was the same age as the character, was crucial to the film's mass-market success.

Once Divine and I got past the initial tension—it didn't help that I had no idea who he was, having never seen a John Waters movie or danced the night away at a gay disco (yet!)—we really clicked. We had so much fun, and we never stopped laughing.

At the same time, Divine was the consummate professional, the person from whom I learned how to be a hard-working actor. Sweat perpetually poured off his brow, a result of unwavering concentration and effort, and although he was the undisputed star of the show, he was all about teamwork. Divine was the opposite of a diva, never complaining about any element of doing his job or anyone else's. He was always in it to help everyone do their best. He knew that the success of a film depended on the relationships between the members of its ensemble, and he never considered himself too important to walk among the "little people." He was both the strongest man I ever knew and the mother I never had.

Divine helped me to feel comfortable in what, besides college, was my first experience away from home. *Hairspray* was my sleepaway camp. It burst my insular bubble. After I'd seen the universe of John Waters, I couldn't wait to get out of the world I had known.

Watching *Hairspray* now, it's amazing to see how convincing Divine was playing my mother. Sure, he was known for his kitsch and camp, but he was really a very natural, believable actor.

In the fall after we wrapped *Hairspray,* but before the movie came out, I went to a few crazy parties at Divine's apartment in New York. His get-togethers were larger than life, just as he was—orgies of food and drink and flirting. Not one to bother with a complicated wardrobe when he wasn't working, he wore giant T-shirts that said "SMILE" in huge block letters. He had them in every color, but their message was redundant. It was impossible not to smile when you were around him.

Divine's place in New York had floor-to-ceiling windows, and it seemed to be overflowing with chocolate-covered strawberries.

"RICKI!" he'd bellow as I walked in the door, and then instead of offering me a drink, he'd say "Let's share a pie! Let's share a roast!" He proclaimed these offers in his unmistakable, musical baritone, gesturing over to the massive buffet spread as I collapsed on the floor with laughter. (He wasn't kidding about the pie, or the roast, and yes, we shared both, more than once.)

Given my less-than-ideal experiences with human sexuality thus far, you might think I would have felt uncomfortable attending Divine's libertine parties. But surprisingly, it was the opposite. Divine and his crew exposed me to the pure joy of individuality. In seeing their happiness, I found a peculiar kind of hope for my own future. I probably felt so safe with Divine and his crew because they were gay men and were neither interested in nor threatening to me.

On March 7, 1988, Divine was in Los Angeles preparing to shoot his first episode of *Married with Children,* the raunchy sitcom that starred a young Christina Applegate. He was thrilled to be playing Al's Uncle Otto—finally, a man.

It was the night before his first day on set—Divine enjoyed an early dinner in Hollywood with friends before turning in for the night. As the evening came to a close, he serenaded his friends by leaning over the hotel balcony and singing "Arrivederci, Roma."

When he didn't show up for work the next morning, Divine's manager went to check on him, and discovered him dead in his hotel room. He was just forty-two years old. Although Divine had been in relatively good health, he weighed over 350 pounds at his autopsy. His heart had failed while he slept.

When John called to tell me what had happened, I was reclining on my rainbow-striped bedspread in Hastings-on-Hudson. I had been living in my childhood room ever since we'd wrapped the movie.

The news came out of nowhere and hit me hard. At that moment, I realized Divine had become like a real father to me. I had just found a proper second parent, and I'd lost him. I understood then, more clearly than I ever had before, that there was nothing left for me at home anymore. I needed to move out on my own.

Traveling down to Baltimore for the funeral, I felt as though I had aged ten years. It was such a surreal situation—every member of *Hairspray*'s cast and crew was there except the most important one. And we weren't making a movie. There was nothing to do but grieve. It was strange to see everybody looking so down, when the mood of John's movies, both on screen and off, is perpetually up.

Divine had walked the red carpet at the opening of our film just a little more than a week earlier, and now we were preparing to put his body into the ground.

At the funeral, John Waters pulled me aside and said, "Honey, I like you fat, I like you thin, but I don't want you dying because of your weight." At that point, I must have been at my highest weight of around 260 pounds. I weighed around 200 while filming *Hairspray*, but I'd been gaining steadily during the eight months since we'd wrapped. Dancing burns a lot of calories, after all.

I had been stuck on a self-esteem roller coaster while shooting *Hairspray*, feeling like a million-dollar ingenue one minute and a dowdy fool the next. I was always looking for an excuse to feel good about myself without having to do any real work: psychological, or physical.

Promoting the film provided me the perfect opportunity to live in total denial of my weight problem. The press loved me! The public seemed to love me, too! If I was America's sweetheart, I couldn't really be *that* fat, right? That *Hairspray* ladies' choice guy was nothing but a judgmental jerk, and everybody else was just jealous that they were extras and I was the star. Who says I'm too fat to be attractive? Not world-famous film director John Waters! Bring on the mozzarella sticks!

While I must have weighed at least 200 pounds during filming, I guess I managed to convince myself, and even my public, that I was much, much smaller. Even *People* magazine was buying my the-camera-adds-50-pounds-not-10 theory, as evidenced in this article published at the time:

> The mashed potato may be food to some, but Lake makes it a feast for the eyes as she shakes and grinds through the old '60s dance. "I'm such a ham," admits the actress. "I always wanted to be Shirley Temple, a little curly top. I dreamed of playing in Annie, but I'm not exactly the starving orphan type."
>
> No, indeed. In fact, the star of director John Waters' coiffure comedy, "Hairspray," is a good

deal more than the average undernourished star-
let. "I'd love to redefine the fat-girl-as-heroine,"
says Lake. Having filled out her 5'3" frame to 150-
plus lbs. during filming, she has done just that.

"Having filled out her frame"? No preparatory weight gain
had been necessary in order for me to play Tracy Turnblad. Still,
if magazines were willing to print my weight as less than it was,
I was willing to believe I weighed less than I actually did. Sure,
I thought of myself as overweight, but not as *fat* per se. It was
just easier to move around the world with confidence if I convinced myself I was normal. I became very fond of citing that
quote about the average American woman being a size 12 or 14,
even though I was much larger.

Everyone marveled at the fact that I'd so happily embraced
my oversized identity: *How evolved I was for such a young girl in
the movie business!* I got a lot of credit for self-acceptance, but
nobody realized I was just fooling myself. I was able to walk
tall because I had somehow tricked myself into thinking that
I didn't have a weight problem.

While I remain eternally grateful for the physical confidence John Waters and everyone else who worked on *Hairspray*
instilled in me when I was an obese and somewhat awkward
teenager, it seems in retrospect that their validation was a mixed
blessing: I came to feel so comfortable with my size that I allowed myself to gain even more weight.

Living in denial took some effort. I deliberately turned
away from mirrors when I walked past them. Once I was no
longer dancing forty hours a week as I had been while filming *Hairspray,* the weight began to pile onto my petite frame,

but I barely noticed. I was used to wearing elastic waists, so my clothing grew with me, which meant that I didn't need to go shopping and confront how big I had gotten. Because I was the star of a hit movie, people stayed interested in me despite the fact that I was careening further and further away from the American beauty ideal and, much more important, away from a state of good health and healthy self-esteem.

I was doing a lot of press in those days. Despite my size, people wanted to read about me.

When I was forced to provide my measurements for a wardrobe fitting—a humiliating ordeal that involved assessing, poking, and prodding my body—I would lie about my size to the costume people or magazine editors. I claimed to be a size 12 or 14 when I was actually at least a 20, too embarrassed to admit that my girth extended way beyond normal sizes and into the realm of "plus," "X," "queen."

In *Hairspray*, my character had been thrilled to be cast as the model for the plus-size clothing store called Hefty Hideaway, modeling metallic shifts while simultaneously devouring pink pastries. But unlike Tracy, Ricki wanted to be thought of as regular size, not plus—no matter what I really looked like. I had my own personal "don't ask, don't tell" policy when it came to my measurements.

Of course, by the time I arrived at the wardrobe fitting having fibbed about my size, not one of the hundreds of garments that hung from the endless rows of rolling racks would fit on my body.

More than once I broke out in hives, totally freaked out about the reality of how big I was getting, worried that someone would know my true size. I don't know whether I thought lying about my size would actually make people believe I was smaller than I looked, but in the magical realm of denial, nothing needs to make sense.

While still living at home in Hastings-on-Hudson, I rode the wave of my *Hairspray* success by appearing in films such as *Cookie* and *Working Girl* and telling funny stories on *The David Letterman Show*. You know, regular teenage girl stuff. Just kidding—I was completely mystified that this fantasy of an existence had become my real life. We shot *Working Girl* the week after *Hairspray* opened, and even though I was barely more than a glorified extra, people on the set treated me like gold. It was perfect timing.

The next fall, I shot a television movie called *Babycakes*, and it aired on CBS the following Valentine's Day. Although my time with the John Waters crew had really loosened me up, it was starring in *Babycakes* that helped me to see myself as a fully formed woman with a sensual side rather than an inexperienced, almost asexual little girl who was happiest hiding under the covers in her childhood bedroom.

Babycakes told the story of Grace, my character, a sweet but seemingly invisible mortician who desperately wants to catch the eye of Rob, a handsome subway conductor. At first, Rob looks right through Grace and into the eyes of his skinny girlfriend, but she—*okay, I*—wins him over with a magic cocktail of home cooking, sparkling personality, and Hollywood magic.

My costar in *Babycakes* was Craig Sheffer, a full-on BABE. Perhaps you know him from his role in *A River Runs Through It* (or maybe *Teen Wolf*; no shame there; I watched it too).

The *Babycakes* script required my character to undergo more sexual experience on screen than I'd yet had in real life, a fact that filled me with shame and terror. What if, once I got on set, I didn't know what to do in bed? What if everybody on the crew thought I was a total idiot or, worse, what if Craig thought I was? What if they laughed at me because I was so sexually inexperienced? How could anyone believe a guy as handsome as Craig would be interested in a girl as fat as me? What if Craig was mind-blowingly disappointed when he realized I was his costar? What if he pulled out of the whole thing?

What if he didn't pull out at all?

Oh wait, right. This was pretend sex. Well, at least I didn't have to worry about getting pregnant.

The apex of my panic came when I read that I'd be expected to take a bubble bath—naked, as most humans tend to do—ON CAMERA.

WITH CRAIG.

Horrifying. I must have been weighing in at around 250 pounds at this point. I wanted to pull out of the whole thing myself. What if my "love interest" was cruel to me? Enduring such intimate cruelty would be ten times more devastating than withstanding the childish antics of my two-faced, fat-phobic love interest from *Hairspray*. No movie role could be worth sacrificing all my hard-earned self-esteem.

Leading up to shooting *Babycakes,* I could break a sweat just by imagining how awkward the bathtub scene was going to be. I worried that my naked body would gross Craig out. Had he ever seen stretch marks or cellulite in his entire life? Of course not! A guy like Craig must be accustomed to women who looked like Malibu Barbie.

And you wouldn't believe how much angst was produced by my contemplating how both of us were going to fit in the bathtub. (Note to self at the time: *Possible to get in tub when it's empty, then proceed with filling? No way to predict water displacement level.*)

Regardless of my anxiety, I knew that the show must go on, and hence, so must I.

I left for Toronto, where we would be shooting on location, in a state of panic and with a strong sense of resolve. I would not let this assignment intimidate me. This was a job—a great job!— and I was in no position to mess it up. The producers wouldn't have cast me if they didn't think I could play the role, and I would do my best to exceed their expectations.

Besides, I *really* needed the money. I was going nuts living in my parents' house, and I had to collect enough cash to get out of there. I would do whatever it took to have my own life, even if it meant humiliating myself in millions of homes across North America and the US Territories.

My first night in Canada was sleepless as I waited to see how I would be received by the *Babycakes* cast and crew. But meeting Craig the next day made me feel infinitely better, pretty much instantly. We had an immediate chemistry, thank God.

Soon after we started speaking candidly to each other, I admitted that I'd been afraid that he might find me repellent.

"WHAT did you say?" Craig replied, with a kind, masculine toughness that let me know everything was going to be okay. Then he took a deep breath and said, with an intensity that let me know he really meant it, "You're a hot woman. That's all there is to it."

Swoon.

Swoonswoonswoon.

I wanted Craig.

Craig did not seem horrified by me.

Okay, maybe he even liked me a little? Could such a thing really be possible?

This was great news! We were both game. Given the way Craig had reassured me, it now seemed highly unlikely that he would run screaming in fear when confronted with my ample flesh.

Still, there was the issue of my sexual inexperience. Not only did I not want to look stupid during filming, but I also didn't want Craig to think he was the only one who found me irresistible. I knew that making everyone believe I had a posse of suitors would add to my allure. So that Craig wouldn't lose interest or doubt his innate attraction to me, I needed him to think I was constantly in demand. Which meant, of course, that he could not find out that I was still a virgin.

How in the world is a virgin, who doesn't want anybody to know she is a virgin, supposed to know how to act when she's asked to simulate sex on camera? (Remember, this was long before the Internet. Back then, porn wasn't so easy to access, study, or emulate.) I felt as though I had to learn another language overnight, and I didn't know anybody who spoke it.

Not only could I not find any X-rated films to watch without going to a creepy store, I also could not Google the straightforward phrase, "how to seem like you've had sex when in fact you have not," because Google did not yet exist. I was on my own here. I didn't have any close girlfriends willing or experienced enough to walk me through the basics. I was fucked. Well actually, I wasn't—and that was the problem.

Finally, it was judgment day. The lights were hot. The bathtub was small. The *Babycakes* crew did all they could to make the whole thing as easy on me as possible. They declared a closed set, which meant only the crew members whose presence was absolutely necessary were allowed in the immediate vicinity of my unmasked flesh. Even then, there was always someone hovering about with a big terrycloth robe, ready to cover me up. I was convinced this was at least as much because the crew didn't want to be forced to witness my naked pulchritude unless absolutely necessary, as it was to preserve my modesty. Profound self-doubt is hard to shake.

With on-camera sex, as with real sex, the buildup is often a bigger deal than the thing itself. By the time I'd finished wrestling with the emotions of it, then tackled the nerves—and by the time they'd finally managed to figure out a plan for our hair and makeup that could withstand copious amounts of steam and sweat, and they'd calibrated precisely the number of bubbles that were needed to hide what must be hid, while still showing what had to be shown—by the time all these little things had been figured out, I was too exhausted to have a panic attack.

Yet despite my newly found sense of calm, I still had a monster crush on Craig, the sort of primal yearning that turns one's heart into a caveman drum. As we sat there in bathrobes, waiting for the director to yell, "Action!" Craig reassured me over and over again that things were bound to go swimmingly. (We were in a bathtub, after all!) I smiled at him, doing my best to appear totally confident. But deep down, I secretly worried that Craig was going to turn on me, causing me profound humiliation in front of everyone. I had been burned before. You know what they say: the first cut is the deepest. Thanks a lot, *Hairspray* Sadie Hawkins guy, for murdering my mojo.

As we were finally directed to embrace and offer the television audience indisputable evidence of our love, Craig could barely get his arms around me. Still, I permitted myself to let whatever squeezing he did manage to accomplish feel really, really good. I forced myself to luxuriate in the moment instead of standing outside the scene and critically observing myself from some point high above. For the first time, I was savoring an experience that forced me to be totally vulnerable instead of squeezing my eyes tight, clenching my fists, and trying to disappear. This bathtub scene marked some serious personal progress.

Should you ever find yourself in the position of having to film a love scene, the most important thing to remember is that you're not the only one who feels awkward. I once saw an interview with Sigourney Weaver where she recounted a costar coming up to her before filming to say, "I'm sorry if I get an erection, and I'm sorry if I don't." That sentence pretty much sums up how everybody participating in a love scene is feeling, no matter whether they're fat or skinny, interested or not.

Babycakes aired on CBS on Valentine's Day 1989. Even though I still struggled mightily with my weight and self-esteem, I was able to accept the film's warm reception as a love letter to myself.

9

I'll never "go Hollywood."

⟊⟊⟊

So now I'd had a hot on-screen boyfriend. Nobody could dispute my attractiveness. I'd been in a couple of really popular movies, and people on the street were starting to know my name. It would have been nice if my neighbors had known it already, but nonetheless, I was finally a big star. In my own mind, anyway. And what do big stars do? They head for the hills. The Hollywood Hills!

I moved from New York to Los Angeles in January 1989 when I was just twenty years old. The first thing I did when I arrived in the kingdom of a thousand freeways was—what else?—buy myself my very own brand-new car.

My chariot was a black Honda Prelude, a tiny Japanese car that was somewhat comically dwarfed by my ample frame—not to mention the fact that getting in and out of that two-door car was a bitch. My Prelude boasted a giant mobile phone, which was attached to the pleather armrest with a curly cord so short that the thing could barely reach my ear while I was driving. For all you John Hughes fans, it was exactly the kind of communication device installed in Jake Ryan's dad's Rolls-Royce in the movie *Sixteen Candles*—a brick with buttons.

So I had a hot car, and I was feeling pretty hot myself, even though some people might have considered me to be as fat as a house. I didn't care. *Look out world, here comes Ricki Lake!* How could you miss me?

I moved to LA not knowing one person, but in my young mind, I was a big movie star, and big movie stars had no trouble making friends. *Hairspray* had been a huge hit, John Waters's most successful film by miles, and John had already asked me to play a sexy pregnant teen in his next movie, *Cry-Baby*, which starred Johnny Depp. I was completely starstruck—by myself. Obsessed with being recognizable, I was really into having made it. (Even though I hadn't really made it yet, of course.)

Almost immediately upon my arrival on the West Coast, I found an apartment in a brand-new building in the middle of Los Angeles, on Detroit Avenue and Fourth Street. I was going to be one of the first people to live in this particular development, and I had my pick of apartments. Like a true diva, I chose to make my home on the top floor, but much to my chagrin, nobody called it "the penthouse." Semantics aside, to me, this place was really cushy; it made me feel R-I-C-H, RICH! I had a one-bedroom with high ceilings, a living room, and a balcony. Although now I'd probably find it dated and disgusting, at the time, my pad filled me with swagger. Yes indeed, I was movin' on up.

Never one to be lonely, I promptly secured myself two fine roommates, kittens I rescued right after I signed my lease. I loved them until I became desperately allergic. When I could no longer tolerate the sneezing, I was forced to give my kitties away, but I still craved a warm touch the way a baby raised in a refrigerator box yearns for human contact. I decided to prowl the wilds of Hollywood for some human companionship.

In my sweet new pad, I planned to welcome adulthood with a bang. Literally. Technically, even though I'd done it on national TV, I was still a virgin—and changing that status was at the top of my to-do list.

I just wanted to get it over with. I set my sights on a handsome fellow named Dustin whom I'd met on the set of *Cry-Baby*. Dustin was the perfect guy to lose my virginity to. He was gorgeous and sweet, and he made me feel remarkably good about myself.

During and after production on *Cry-Baby*, Dustin and I hung out a lot. Looking back at photographs from the time, I can tell that we were genuinely fond of each other, despite our aesthetic incompatibility. What do I mean by "aesthetic incompatibility"? Well, let's just say that lying on the floor of my apartment together, playing video games, Dustin and I looked like Gumby and Ms. Pac-Man caught in a moment of interspecies infatuation. By no means were Dustin and I "in love," but we were both interested in exploring each other's sensuality. Basically, neither of us was opposed to fooling around.

I decided to lose my virginity to Dustin because I was really dying to be normal. I was twenty years old, and it was time. At that point I probably would have done it with anybody, to be honest, but I was glad I had found an inarguably hot guy who seemed like he'd be nice to me the morning after, even if he wasn't exactly my intellectual equal.

Looking back on memories of him now, I realize Dustin possessed another wonderful human quality in addition to his kindness: a really big dick. At that point in my sexual life. I had no other specimens with which to compare Dustin's impressive—ahem, "member"?—but in hindsight, what God didn't give him in the penthouse, he gave him on other floors.

I was nervous about getting naked that first time with Dustin. He didn't really bother much with foreplay—no soft gestures, no kind words. I don't really doubt that he liked me, but I'm not sure how attracted he was to me in particular.

Sleeping with Dustin, I was not yet connected enough to my own body to even hope of achieving an orgasm. I was, however, connected to each and every friend whose phone number I had within ten minutes of completing the act. I left my conquest sleeping in the bedroom while I ran into the living room to activate the phone tree.

The fact that I was more excited about the telling my friends I'd had sex than the having sex itself is just one example of how confused I was when it came to getting in touch with my own sexuality. Why was I so keen on telling my friends immediately? Because I thought the news proved I wasn't a freak after all. I thought the only way to convince my friends, and myself, that I was sexually appealing was to offer concrete evidence that I had appealed to someone sexually. The point was, I never really knew where I stood. Some days I thought I was attractive;

other days, I knew I was disgusting. Neither one of these opinions was grounded in an objective sense of self, but in the ways random people looked at me, and the offhand things they said.

Even now, my friends always tell me that I was attractive even when I was heavy. They say, "Get off it, Ricki. You were an international movie star! Everybody thought you were beautiful. They must have, or you wouldn't have gotten as huge as you did." (No pun intended. Or maybe it was?)

The important thing was that I didn't *feel* beautiful. Not in a calm, self-confident, sexually alluring, quintessentially feminine way. I knew I was magnetic, sure, but in order to hold my value, I felt that I needed to be constantly onstage, forever trying to sell everyone on my worth. Like if I didn't work hard enough to convince people to love me, they'd never come to feeling that way on their own. This left me feeling perpetually exhausted, depleted by my desperation to please, and in a constant state of doubt about everyone's true feelings.

I've often been told—by friends, therapists, boyfriends— that I need to come to terms with the fact that it's possible for me to be attractive at any weight. Those close to me insist that I must accept the fact that my appeal is not necessarily dictated by the harsh, judgmental dichotomy of thin = hot, fat = not. I've never really been able to believe this myself, though, because of the way my weight affects my self-esteem.

Some people say that packing on the pounds can suffocate your sexuality, and this was certainly true for me. I just didn't feel sexual when I was heavy. Maybe I came across on the outside as a voluptuous, ripe young woman, but inside I felt almost neutered.

I believe the reason I wanted to feel that way was to block

out what Joe had done to me when I was a child. One of the main reasons I wanted to lose my virginity—to get the whole thing out of the way—was that I didn't want to enter adulthood feeling as though I were damaged goods. Losing my virginity seemed to offer some sort of fresh start. I think I always held onto a dark fear, even though I didn't really talk about it: I worried that Joe's hands had marked me forever.

Despite being weirdly anticlimactic (no pun intended), I do think that sleeping with Dustin made me feel normal. Despite the absence of fireworks or true love, that night marked a turning point. Losing my virginity was such an important step in my sexual development that about a year later, I began to talk about the abuse that had been done to me.

The guy I found myself able to confide in was my friend Aidan, a gorgeous actor with a sensitive spirit. He was funny. He was smart. And I was kind of in love with him. He eventually turned out to be gay, so it makes sense that I felt safe confiding my deepest, darkest secrets to him. I could just sense that he was never going to hurt me sexually or threaten me in any way.

"Hey Aidan," I whispered one night.

"Yes, Ricki?" he asked.

"When I was six, I was sexually abused."

Hearing the words come out of my mouth was almost an out-of-body experience. *Had I actually told him?*

Aidan's response was kind and consoling. "You are not alone," he told me, and hearing it really helped. Aidan didn't run away from me in fear when I told him about the abuse. What Joe had done to me didn't disgust him or change his fundamental opinion of who I was as a person. He was appropriately shaken and wonderfully kind. "Oh Ricki," he said, "I am so sorry that happened to you."

Until I told Aidan what Joe had done, I hadn't even admitted it had happened to me. My family had still never spoken about it. For years, my only reminder of the trauma that had taken place was this gnawing fear in the back of my mind: *Maybe there's something really wrong. What if I'm never able to become a truly sexual person because of what was done to me?*

Now that my secret had streamed out of me like steam from the top of a boiling kettle, I was starting to feel ready to pour myself into life on my own terms.

10

I'll never make it to the Oscars.

———

Soon after moving to Los Angeles, I got a killer job. Not a *paying* job—a girl has to have *something* to strive for—but a high-exposure offer to perform in a musical number on the Academy Awards. Yes, THAT Academy Awards.

Try to imagine anything more exciting to a graduate of teen cabaret and the Professional Children's School—a kid utterly addicted to Broadway—than appearing in a musical theater number live on national television. For a good forty-six hours after I was asked to do the show, my mouth was basically frozen open like Macaulay Culkin's, that kid in *Home Alone*.

That year, the Academy Awards show was being choreographed by Kenny Ortega. At that moment in 1989, Kenny was on fire, having just choreographed the monster hits *Ferris Bueller's Day Off* and *Dirty Dancing*. Is there anything better than Matthew Broderick dancing atop a parade float to "Danke Schoen," except Jennifer Grey leaping fearlessly into Patrick Swayze's sinewy clutches onstage in the Catskills? You can thank Kenny for both those moments. These days you can catch Mr. Ortega judging *So You Think You Can Dance,* and, of course, directing a series of films for Disney about some kids who perform musical numbers all over the halls of their high school. (Yep, *those High School Musicals.*)

Kenny cast a bunch of up-and-coming performers to be featured in the 1989 Oscar telecast. It would be the television event of the year starring Christian Slater, Savion Glover, Patrick Dempsey, Blair Underwood, the late Carrie Hamilton, Melora Hardin, and many others . . .

ME!

I thought I had died and gone to heaven. Here I was, working with all these people I idolized, and it felt just like putting on a theater camp show. All my training had not been in vain. I was prepared with a capital "P." I hadn't endured those mean theater teachers for nothing.

Looking back, I suppose what we were called on to do was undeniably cheesy (poor Rob Lowe; it took him twenty years to get people to forget that "Snow White" number), but I didn't think what we were doing was at all cheesy at the time. I considered it to be entertainment with a capital "E." I was THE ENCHANTING RICKI LAKE, an ENTERTAINER on NATIONAL TELEVISION!

Maybe I was fat as could be, but I got to sing and dance my heart out, and now the whole world would be watching. Here I was, having it all! *Kiss my ass, naysayers. Tune in Monday night,*

*Toukie Weinstein. In your face, Ithaca College. I'll see you on TV.
Or, rather, you'll see me.*

Thing was, though, I had to find something to wear that
would cover my rapidly expanding physique. On national television. Sigh. There was no time to diet, exercise, or invest in one of
those weight-loss suits.

In addition to performing at the show, Kenny had asked
me to be his date to the Academy Awards ceremony and parties.
Even in a normal city like Chicago or Philadelphia, I would have
had a hard time finding something formal that fit my body. But
in Beverly Hills, plus-sizes are basically unspeakable. Really,
don't mention them. Nobody wants to hear it.

I don't know whether I was clueless or cruelly self-
punishing, but when I embarked on the hunt for my Oscar
getup, I started off at the famous Fred Segal Santa Monica.
Fred Segal is a collection of quirky, expensive boutiques cor-
raled alongside one another in one building, to form a super-
hip department store. It's a legendary clothing emporium that
caters to Hollywood starlets who spend so much time perfect-
ing their sinewy bodies they don't really need to wear clothes at
all. A size 8 woman is made to feel obese at Fred Segal, so you
can imagine how I felt with my own size being more than twice
that.

Now, I know what you might be thinking:

*What amazing self-esteem she had, that Ricki Lake, to be
able to saunter right into such an intimidating place and show
those snooty shopgirls who's boss!*

Nope. To put it quite simply, I was still in denial.

A merchant and wardrobe stylist named Jackie—she later

became a good friend of mine—saw me wandering the mini-shops within Fred Segal, discouraged and pathetically unable to find anything that could even come close to fitting my oversized frame. I felt a sense of relief as her empathetic face approached me. Jackie herself was a big woman—not *heavy-heavy*, in fact she'd just lost a lot of weight, but nonetheless big—and she said, "Don't worry, Ricki. I think I might have something in my personal wardrobe that would fit you."

To paraphrase Blanche DuBois, what the hell would we do without the kindness of strangers? One minute I was red-faced and sweaty, nearly in tears because I thought I'd have to forfeit the Oscars or appear in a Hefty bag. The next minute, glamorous Jackie was inviting me over to her house to try on scads of super-sized designer clothes. Jackie generously lent me what I ended up wearing on the show, a giant tuxedo that branded me as the comic relief in a sea of singing and dancing starlets. It was big, and it was black, and I had arrived in it, both literally and figuratively.

At least you weren't in denial anymore. Once you had to go to someone's house in order to find something big enough to wear, you must have realized your weight was out of control, right? YOU COULD NOT BUY ANYTHING OFF THE RACK AT A REGULAR STORE. The writing was on the wall.

Nope. Shopping was hard, but in spite of it all, I thought, "Eh! I'm still adorable! I couldn't possibly look as fat as I actually am!"

I was positively unsinkable. Had the entertainment thing not worked out, I could have made a career of teaching a Learning Annex course in self-brainwashing to people who wanted to forget they were fat. I had effortlessly mastered this powerful coping mechanism starting all the way back in high school. It worked very well at the time, and so did I.

Thankfully, I experienced no wardrobe malfunctions or devastating humiliations at the Academy Awards. Going to the whole shebang with Kenny Ortega was like being Cinderella at the ball. That Oscar show remains, to this day, one of the most exciting nights of my life. As I scurried across the massive stage in my tuxedo during the goofy song-and-dance number, I actually made eye contact with Tom Hanks, who was watching from the front row. It's a miracle I didn't forget my steps entirely.

How could all this be real? Was it really possible that Tom Hanks was watching me? Wasn't I supposed to be watching him?

After the awards ceremony was over, I got to hang out in the VIP green room, where I sat next to Meg Ryan. Then, as I was walking around backstage, I noticed someone who looked just like Tom Cruise having a conversation with someone and pointing in my direction. This whole thing was so surreal. First I see Meg Ryan, and now here's this guy who's a double for Tom Cruise? *People in Hollywood are so ridiculously good looking. Have I gotten trapped in* Top Gun?

The lookalike and I made eye contact, and he motioned for me to come over to where he was standing. "I loved you in *Hairspray*," this strong-jawed, twinkle-eyed man said. Once I heard his voice, it was undeniable: this was no lookalike.

Take my breath away, indeed. I couldn't believe it. I was absolutely stunned that Tom Fucking Cruise knew who I was.

But then a tiny part of me wasn't *so* surprised.

11

I'll never feel at home anywhere.

In order to survive the making of *Hairspray*, I learned to psych myself out of being self-conscious. I had to play mind games. I'd say to myself, *Well, they hired me to be the girl that gets the guy, so that means that's who I am, in the real world as well as on-screen. I am so spectacular a human being that I always get the guy, even though I'm fat! The regular Hollywood rules simply do not apply to me!*

I managed to convince myself that I was happy with the way I looked, but this didn't mean I could tolerate the sight of myself naked. I had to preserve my delusion somehow. I couldn't stop myself from feeling fat, though. The physical signs were impossible to ignore: I was so top-heavy that by the end of the day, I'd have ridges in my shoulders from the constant pulling of my bra straps.

If you look at images of me from *China Beach*, the TV drama on which I appeared at my highest weight of approximately 260 pounds, I had virtually no neck, and my boobs were up to here and down to there.

Waist? Not. Want? Not.

Still, with my new apartment and new Hollywood friends, I was sitting pretty. I had a fantastic social life: the attendance list for my twenty-first birthday party read like a *People* magazine crossword. And even though I couldn't fit into the floral-print, spaghetti-strap dresses that were so popular at the time, I had a tremendous hat collection and drawers spilling over with really cute ankle socks.

In addition to hats, I'd begun collecting famous friends. My twenty-first birthday party was all about having as many famous people as I could gather in one place to celebrate . . . ME!

And my celebration did not disappoint. The little karaoke bar inside the Japanese restaurant we had reserved for the occasion was not only overflowing with sake, but also with late-1980s pop icons. Sarah Jessica Parker, Eve Plumb from *The Brady Bunch*, the cast of *China Beach*, Christian Slater, Matthew Perry, Marlee Matlin, Cindy Gibb, Marg Helgenberger—all these fabulous folks showed up to toast me into adulthood.

Crazy as it may sound, I felt more nurtured in my new life in Hollywood than I had at home in Hastings-on-Hudson. Out in California, people weren't afraid to share their feelings about themselves or for one another. Once presented with emotional intimacy and unapologetic frankness, I realized I had long been craving it, even though I'd never had a taste before.

The member of this crowd to whom I became—and

stayed—closest was Mandy Ingber, who at the time was an actress, and now has a career as a well-known yoga and fitness personality.

I first met Mandy at an audition for the television show *Silver Spoons*, but when we ran into each other for a second time, she didn't remember me. Instead of feeling insulted, I took her slight as a challenge. Mandy and I soon became constant, if unlikely, companions. She was thin with kinky curls, while I was chubby with slick, straight tresses. But we had a lot in common: we shared our Jewish identities, our boundless founts of energy, and our wry senses of humor. Most of all, we shared a love for eating. Unlike me, Mandy was skinny. But this didn't mean she didn't still like to eat.

A lot.

Our favorite thing to do was stake out a good table at Souplantation, an all-you-can-eat chain restaurant situated right across the street from the Beverly Center—the mall in Tom Petty's "Free Fallin'" video—and park ourselves there for the day.

We'd put out an all-points bulletin to our friends—this was before the days of cell phones, so I guess we must have done it by carrier pigeon or tin can—that we were holding court "in front of the yogurt machine," or "behind the muffin bar" or whatever. We'd pay for just one lunch plate each and sit there noshing all day long like it was our office. The place was so cheap that our room and board there probably worked itself out to be about 10 cents an hour.

Because Souplantation prided itself on being "healthy" in that delusional carb-loving eighties fashion—all massive muffins and low-fat pasta "salads"—we weren't ashamed to put tons of food away. I wasn't, anyway. I was ravenous, too busy eating to notice that most of my friends spent all day playing with the same plate of food while I kept replenishing mine.

I didn't have to eat at Souplantation for long.

Hanging out with all these Young Hollywooders must have rubbed off on me somehow. Just months after moving to LA, I was offered a recurring role on ABC's award-winning drama, *China Beach*.

My character, Holly Pelegrino, was a feisty volunteer for the Red Cross whose main duties involved the distribution of breakfast pastries, with a liberal garnish of flirtation. Yes, that's right, folks: I was a "Donut Dolly." It's possible that, in agreeing to play the role of Holly, I was reinforcing negative fat-girl stereotypes. Still, I was proud of myself for winning the role. So what if I didn't have a perfect body? I was making it in Hollywood. I was breaking the mold for what it meant to be a leading lady. I was blazing trails.

And when it came to my salary, I wasn't dealing with John Waters's movie budget anymore. This was network prime time, people. The minute after I signed my deal, I started house hunting. (I already had the car.)

I moved out of my rented apartment in Hollywood and into my very own home in Nichols Canyon, off LA's famous Mulholland Drive. I paid almost three-quarters of a million dollars for the privilege of being a homeowner, throwing down every penny of my savings—about $180,000 in cash—as a down payment.

My little house had three bedrooms and three-and-a-half bathrooms. It was adorable and girly and painted robin's egg blue, and driving up to it at the end of a long day proved I had really made it. Although I didn't have a piece of furniture (no cash left to buy any), I decorated my house with people. And it looked absolutely amazing.

12

I'll never lose my own home.

Although I was making money working on *China Beach*, I wasn't keeping any. My first business manager—the one who had encouraged me to buy a house as soon as I was able—failed to teach me anything about how to manage my finances. Note to those of you just getting cast on a hit network television series: wait until you've shored up the details of your contract before signing any loan papers.

When I made nowhere near as much money on *China Beach* as I had been promised, I turned to my parents for help paying my mortgage, so I wouldn't lose the house I'd worked so hard to buy. My dad floated me for six months, but even that turned out to be for nought when my contract with *China Beach* was not renewed, and I scrambled, but I was unable to find a job that would put me back on my feet.

I lost my perfect little house and my perfect little life, not to mention six months' worth of mortgage payments borrowed from my father's hard-earned savings. At this point, I was at my fattest. Around 260 pounds, I think, but you can bet I was going nowhere near the scale in those days. There was nothing to do but retreat to the suburbs with my tail between my legs.

Which were, of course, rubbing together.

Given that the waif look was in, there weren't that many roles that fit me. Just when I thought I was destined to return to Hastings-on-Hudson—maybe teach some drama at Ithaca College?—I was overjoyed to learn I'd been cast in an NBC pilot. I threw myself into the job, agreeing to take time to meet with every actress the producers were considering casting around me. Little did I know that after the endless stream of auditions I was forced to endure, I would be the one replaced.

Once a major movie star in my own mind, I was now seriously unemployed. I would have to pare down my living situation in order to survive.

I started my new life by subletting a tiny pool house nestled deep in the San Fernando Valley. I handed over my rent check each month to a lovely elderly lady named Anne Klein. I decided to take a new approach to my career: now that my costs were low, instead of seeking out whichever projects brought the biggest paychecks, I would fight for the work that most interested me. I had nothing to lose.

You might think that *not* getting cast as a homely girl who spends an entire motion picture being made fun of behind her back—and then to her face—would be a compliment. Not for me. Losing out on an "ugly" role was a huge blow to my self-esteem.

This reaction actually marked real personal growth for me. Instead of staying stuck in my own self-loathing, I was now able to acknowledge that Hollywood was the one with the weight problem.

Do you remember the 1992 movie *Dogfight*? It's the story of three marines who stop over in San Francisco on their way to fight in Vietnam. They decide to spend their last night on US soil picking up three girls who will (unknowingly) compete against one another in a "dog fight," a.k.a. an ugliest-date competition.

The main character, played by River Phoenix, encounters a plain—but by no means ugly—girl named Rose in a coffee shop, where she works as a waitress. Eddie comes on to Rose because he thinks she'll make the winning ugly date. But the two soon develop a poignant chemistry and Eddie is filled with regret as he realizes what he has done. He tries to shake Rose off numerous times throughout their long evening together so she doesn't have to find out why he was drawn to her in the first place. But she's so enthralled with him that she can't take a hint, and he doesn't admit to anything. Their connection is so real, so rare, so effortless, that he can't bring himself to tell her the truth.

Eddie takes the risk of bringing Rose to the bar where the dog fight will be (clandestinely) judged. He has to meet back up with his friends after all. Rose finds out why Eddie approached her in the first place. Although she fails to be named ugliest date, she is devastated by what she believes to be Eddie's true feelings.

However, Eddie and Rose's connection is so strong that

they, however implausibly, spend the rest of the evening together. And although they talk about their dreams for the future, any sense of youthful hopefulness is overshadowed by the
war Eddie is about to fight and the cruel misogyny that brought
him and Rose together.

At the end of the night, Eddie and Rose share an awkward
but tender sexual experience. Eddie goes off to war and Rose
lives a quiet life in San Francisco. When Eddie returns three
years later, humbled by a limp and the loss of his friends in com-
bat, he finds Rose now running the café where she used to work
as a waitress. With him now broken and her now strong, the end
of the movie implies that Eddie and Rose will embark on a new,
honest relationship not marred by their imperfections but made
stronger for them.

Good story, right? Well, that's what I thought. After reading just a few lines, I couldn't put it down. Rose was a complex
character: she was smart, she was strong, she was funny, she
was resilient. I believed, on the inside, that we were alike. And
there was, of course, the most significant quality we shared: as
originally written in the script I read, the character of Rose was
described as "fat."

I don't need to tell you how difficult it is for women to find
good roles in Hollywood, much less how hard it is to discover
overweight characters who are drawn in nuanced strokes rather
than in gross caricature. Parts like Rose come along once in a
lifetime. I recognized the specialness of *Dogfight* immediately,
and I vowed to make the role mine.

Reading *Dogfight* made me believe that I could be taken seriously one day—as more than just a mascot. Rose was evidence

that Hollywood could acknowledge the complexities of being a woman who struggles to exist within social norms. *Dogfight* provided evidence that an entertaining film can engage in real social issues. It reminded me that great art can make a difference. I was exhilarated at the prospect of being part of something that could change opinions, maybe even lives.

I prepared for my *Dogfight* audition as I had never prepared for an audition before. I read and reread the script, really trying to get inside Rose's head, making her character my own. Once it was time for me to meet with the film's director, I already identified deeply with Rose's every aspect. Behind the closed door of that casting session, I gave the performance of my life, breaking down and connecting to both pain and strength deep inside myself. I emerged from the room shaking with the adrenaline of victory, absolutely sure that I'd gotten the part.

A few days later, I learned that I had not. Rose, written as a girl who was charming but quite overweight, had been changed into an awkward, mousy type with a Hollywood body. A pretty, thin girl named Lili Taylor had been given the role, and I was made to feel like a fool for even throwing my hat in the ring.

My feelings of devastation at failing to get cast in *Dogfight* had as much to do with mourning the invisibility of overweight women in American cinema as it did with feeling sorry for myself because of a career setback. I guess it was a small personal victory that I was overwhelmed more by a sense of social injustice—*Doesn't Hollywood realize that the Roses of the world look like me?*—than with frustration over the state of my own career.

Still, I was starting to feel that in order to stay relevant,

I was going to have to reinvent myself. And deep down I realized that was probably going to mean losing weight.

⌒⌒⌒

Losing the role in *Dogfight* marked a turning point for me—the moment when I realized that I needed to reinvent myself. Any honest celebrity will tell you that having a successful career is all about creating a gimmick. As a performer, you have to constantly ask yourself, *What sets me apart? What makes me stand out?* You're not so much a person as a product. A product that you need the public to keep buying, over and over again—and only you can give them a reason to do so.

I'd been fat for a really long time. I wouldn't have blamed anyone for having grown sick of me. I knew I needed to change everything about myself in order to be relevant again. So I made a conscious decision to embark on a no-holds-barred mission of self-transformation. *Okay, Hollywood, so you're sick of fat Ricki? Wait until you get a load of skinny Ricki! And then let's see if she gives you a second look!*

In 1990, *New York Times* writer Janet Maslin had this to say about my appearance in John Waters's *Cry-Baby:*

> Players in *Cry-Baby* embody various degrees of freakishness, some of it way off the charts. Kim McGuire, as the hideously contorted floozy called Hatchet-Face, is too frightening to be funny, and the same can be said for Susan Tyrrell as *Cry-Baby*'s trampy grandma. Closer to the middle of the spectrum is the sporting Ricki Lake,

Mr. Waters's plump *Hairspray* star, who is here supposed to be pregnant.

"*Who is here **supposed** to be pregnant.*"

As if John were trying to apologize away my weight by giving my character another reason to carry it besides lifestyle or metabolism. As if all fat characters are the same, so how many times can we possibly tolerate them over and over again?

I was sick of people feeling that way about me. Even more, I was sick of feeling that way about myself. That all I was was "that famous fat girl." And that was no longer enough.

13

I'll never get thin.

Mine is not your typical celebrity weight-loss tale. I didn't hire a trainer. I ended up dating one for a long time years later and I slept with a couple of others (but that's another story). I didn't get gastric bypass. They barely even had it back in my day, but even if the procedure had been available, I'm sure I would have been too broke or too squeamish to try it.

What did I do in order to get thin, then? I decided I'd finally had it with the current state of my life. I went on a serious crash diet without telling anybody what I was up to. I made all these crazy major life changes in secret. I decided to keep my new way of life to myself because I had failed at losing weight so many times before, and the last thing I needed was to humiliate myself by breaking a promise nobody really believed I'd be able to keep in the first place.

My highly glamorous Hollywood weight-loss plan involved breast reduction, a bicycle, a supermarket loyalty card, and a branch of 24 Hour Fitness nestled deep in the San Fernando Valley. Since I had no money to speak of and a kitchen that consisted of just a bar sink and a hot plate, I figured that I had arrived at an excellent time in my life to try my hand at a starvation diet.

To be fair, I think it was having a breast reduction that really jump-started my weight-loss success. Since the age of fourteen, when I seemed to undergo puberty over the course of a three-day weekend, my breasts had ruled my life. My cleavage was like a wavy river flowing from my chin to the bottom of my bra strap. My shoulders were permanently marred by deep, angry grooves left behind by undergarments working overtime, and the valley down the middle of my back, between my shoulder blades, was permanently sore. My boobs were so big, I literally looked as though I had no neck. They rose up to my chin and sank down to my waist. I am only 5'3" so my entire top half was composed of boob. Even though they represented major, major surgery, I found the words "breast reduction" neither unfamiliar nor terrifying. Both my mother and sister had already had the procedure, so I suppose I always believed it inevitable that I would follow suit.

It was no secret that my breasts were very, very big. In *Hairspray,* I wore a 44DD bra. This was not because I had been fit properly and 44DD was my size, but because 44DD was the biggest bra size carried by a regular store. I couldn't bear the idea of willfully submitting to the tape measure of some skinny Victoria's Secret saleswoman, only to be told, with an eye roll, that she was terribly sorry, but her store didn't service—ahem—

assets as large as mine. Shouldering my melons wasn't all bad, though. As a "fat actress," their size had always worked in my favor, keeping the proportions between my chest and my abdomen pleasantly feminine despite my girth.

I committed to changing my silhouette completely, so I wasn't sorry to see those unwieldy breasts go. I went into surgery brimming with excitement, surprisingly unfettered by fear. When I came to, I experienced no remorse. I felt thrilled to have kissed those mamas good-bye and replaced them with some pert little babies. As soon as I felt well enough to move around, I jumped on the scale and discovered that I had lost an amazing seven pounds without even trying.

What if I did try? I wondered to myself. I had pretended to try so many times before, but if I was truly honest with myself, I had to admit that I'd never really committed. Before, though, I'd never really *had* to. People liked me just fine the way I was. My need for personal reinvention had never been this intense. This time, it wasn't about being healthier, or happier, or finding some other sane, emotionally sound reason to lose weight. It was about taking care of myself financially. I knew I needed to get a job, and soon.

Everything in my life was totally out of control, but I had found something to be the boss of. I could control what I put in my mouth and how frequently I chose to move my body.

And for the first time, I believed these changes might actually add up to something major: a new me.

14

A gay man could never really hurt me.

Here's a quick side note. It's a teensy bit disingenuous for me to claim that 100 percent of my motivation in finally losing weight was financial. I also did it to get this guy to like me.

At the time I hit rock bottom, I had become involved in an unhealthy, essentially abusive relationship. This was no coincidence. I doubt I would have wasted a moment of my life pining over this particular boyfriend if I had anything else at all going on. But my self-esteem was at an all-time low, and I was out to fall in love with someone who would hurt me so I didn't have to go through the trouble of doing it myself.

My friend Aidan was a drop-dead-gorgeous actor. He had rich, dark hair, deep blue eyes, and a body that didn't quit. He was in perfect shape, but he didn't look as if he had to try too hard in order to get there. His boy-next-door looks took my breath away. Aidan embodied all the qualities of the sort of men I'd always longed for, but who had looked right through me, time and time again, to someone blonder, thinner, cooler, colder.

Being in a relationship with Aidan was a little bit like playing house. He came over and hung out with me at Anne Klein's. We went swimming, watched TV, lay around on top of each other like teenagers. "Nice boyfriend," everyone would say to me, either with congratulations or suspicion, but I took them at their word. He was.

Looking back, I realize I must have known that Aidan was gay. But at the time we were together, I was so heavy and he was so closeted that I believed he wasn't attracted to me because of my size. I didn't blame him for being turned off by me physically. He said he really loved me, and I believed him. He was sorry, he said, but I was simply too heavy to fuck. He just couldn't get it up for such a fat girl. It was nothing personal.

Despite his cruelty, I let Aidan stick around, and we had fascinating, intense conversations about the most personal parts of our lives. Remember, he had been the first one whom I had told about being abused by Joe. While our relationship wasn't primarily sexual, Aidan and I did fool around in a very innocent, teenager-y kind of way.

I guess some would think it pretty cruel on Aidan's part to let me go on thinking it was my weight, and not my gender, that repelled him. But I got a bit of insight reading about his take on our relationship in a memoir he wrote many years later. In the book, he described me quite fondly—talking about how much fun we had together—and expressed how disappointed he was in himself that he was unable to cultivate a sexual attraction to me. *Why couldn't I let my life be perfect?* This was the question he asked himself. *Because I was imperfect.* Sad.

Probably in part because of his emotional and physical distance, I was absolutely mad for Aidan and totally devastated that he never returned my affections. I've heard armchair psychologists say that women who have been sexually abused are more likely to pine for gay men than women who have not been abused, presumably because they, even if only subconsciously, put out a very safe physical vibe.

I don't really think that's what my thing for Aidan was about, though. Plain and simple, I've always been into hot guys, and Aidan was HOT.

No, my thing with Aidan wasn't safe at all—certainly not emotionally. At one point during our relationship, I was so caught up in love with Aidan, trying so desperately to get him to be physical with me, that during a heated conversation, he snapped. We were standing in Anne Klein's pool house. I was in the kitchen area.

"Why don't you want to touch me?" I screamed at Aidan. "What is wrong with you? We love each other. I don't understand. I want you so badly!"

Hearing these desperate words, Aidan got angry. I watched his face flush red with anger. His mind seemed to be lost somewhere else. His body took on a violent tension, and all of a sudden I found myself afraid of him. I must have known then—as I know now—that his anger wasn't directed at me, but at himself.

Aidan was overwhelmed by frustration. Whether it was toward me for representing all the things that were "wrong" with him or only toward himself, Aidan was simmering with a tragic anger. I can only imagine that his feelings resulted from his pretending to be someone he wasn't for such a long time.

Although Aidan was able to snap out of that intense anger, I was devastated and humiliated by the contempt he had no longer been able to hide. For years I never told anyone about the way Aidan had exploded at me, mostly because I thought the whole thing was bizarre and embarrassing, and it made me seem nothing short of pathetic.

Not only did I not discuss this event with any of my friends, but I also didn't bring it up with Aidan. I've never been one to provoke confrontation or suggest openly talking about something controversial. Given my temperament, I suppose it wouldn't have been difficult to see me as the perfect beard. I attribute my fear of bringing difficult things out in the open to the environment I was raised in. We never spoke about anything painful or important, instead choosing to let anger, awkwardness, and doubt hang in the air like smog until the wind carried them away.

For years, I struggled with trying to understand why Aidan felt such anger toward me. Unlike the really damaging male figures in my life—Joe and Mario—Aidan had never tried to violate me sexually. I should have felt totally safe around him, and yet, I didn't.

Truth be told, I should really be grateful that Aidan was gay. It was because he wasn't sexually attracted to me that I finally decided to lose weight.

In the time I was losing weight, I started to really think about the reasons I was fat in the first place. There's no question that enduring the abuse and then being forced to swallow the experience led to my eating maniacally, putting on weight for comfort and protection. My own family offered me no emotional support at all when it came to dealing with what had happened. It was almost as though what Joe had done to me had barely registered on their radar.

In fact, many years later, by the time I finally broached the subject of what Joe had done to me with my sister, Jennifer, we were full-grown adults. I wanted to know what her own impressions had been of what had happened to me, whether Mom or Dad had explained anything to her, or even warned her about Joe, for the sake of her own safety.

To my total shock, Jennifer told me that she had known nothing about what Joe had done to me when she was in first grade and I was in second. "Oh! Is that why Mom and Dad let you stay home that day, even though you weren't sick?" she asked.

My mother may be lots of things, but she is not a dummy. She must have blamed herself, at least in part, for my weight problem, especially after what had happened with Joe while she was right there in the very same house. And I'm sure the weight of responsibility pushed heavily on my dad as well. But instead of my parents expressing their sadness about what I'd gone through—how sorry they were, how inadequate they felt in their inability to protect me—they stayed silent, pretending that nothing had ever happened.

I suppose it's possible they believed the trauma hadn't affected me—that my success and happy-go-lucky demeanor proved that I was fine. But it would have meant the world to me if they'd told me how strong they thought I was instead of staying silent. Now I see that the whole thing might have simply been too much for them to deal with, but at the time, their silence told me that they simply didn't care.

While I was undergoing my physical transformation, my parents began their own spiritual one, converting from cultural Judaism to born-again Christianity. Maybe one of the reasons my parents were so attracted to Christianity was that it absolved them of the guilt of what had happened to me and how they had refused to handle it.

Another contributing factor came in the form of a terrible crime committed against my father. My father was a second-generation pharmacist who had long had his own business in the Inwood section of Manhattan. After many years of doing the same thing every day, his routine was as regular as clockwork: twice a week, he left the store and walked over to the bank, briefcase in hand, to make a deposit.

One afternoon as he was carrying that deposit envelope, my father was beaten viciously over the head and then robbed. Someone who worked for him must have taken note of his routine and then planned the job.

While my father was being rushed to the hospital in an ambulance, he flatlined—meaning, technically, that he was dead for a moment.

My mother was so shaken up by the whole experience, she declared that she was leaving New York for Las Vegas, whether my father agreed to come or not. Nice way to focus on the healing process of the patient, right? She exhibited the same selfish behavior again many years later when my dad suffered a mysterious brain illness: she disappeared, leaving Jennifer and me to care for him and leaving him without the emotional support of his wife. I'd like to give my mother the benefit of the doubt, saying that she just couldn't tolerate the pain and fear she felt when seeing a loved one in mortal danger, but I'm not convinced she's capable of experiencing the feeling of compassion. She came from a very cold family, and it showed.

After he had recovered, my dad agreed to move to Vegas to join my mother. He sold his pharmacy, then they packed up the house, and moved west for good. There are lots and lots of evangelical Christian congregations in Vegas. My mother had joined one of them upon arriving there, and my father joined her. The Jewish Lakes from Hastings-on-Hudson had become the Christian Lakes of Nevada. My father began to believe that Jesus had saved his life after the beating. He swore that he had died, and then he had been born again.

I'd never felt particularly Jewish. Aside from looking for the hidden matzo at my grandparents' house on Passover and occasionally lighting Hanukkah candles, our family lived a completely secular existence. I mean, we had a Christmas tree. Not to say we knew anything about Jesus—we thought Santa was the patron saint of Christmas. I don't have many memories of family rituals, but Christmas morning, for the Lakes, was really special. My mom wrapped tons of presents; she even cooked. It was during Christmas that I felt the most taken care of and nurtured, one of the only times I truly remember her mothering us. Our Jewish identity was purely cultural. Still, it was something that made our little family part of a greater tradition. I didn't realize it at the time, but I think my family's Jewishness was important to me. If the four of us didn't exactly seem like a bulletproof unit, I could at least look to this broader group for connections. When they abandoned their cultural identity, it seemed like they were admitting we'd failed as a family.

Their new life in Las Vegas seemed totally foreign, and I wondered, deep down, whether they were excluding me on purpose.

15

I'll never be given my own talk show.

∽

With my parents' bizarre religious behavior solidifying my sense of total separation from my family of origin, I was finally able to push through the pain of reaching my goal weight in the hopes of making it on my own—for real, this time.

After a year of self-deprivation and a weight loss of over 100 pounds, I was ready for my new life to begin. Even so, I was surprised when it did. One ordinary morning, I got a call from a friend of a friend asking me to audition for a new daytime talk show that was being developed to target a younger audience. I was skeptical. Who was this dude, and how had he gotten my home number? What if this was a prank?

After thinking things through a bit, I figured the audition was probably legit, considering the guy had told me to show up at the Twentieth Century Fox studio lot. Besides, I didn't have anything better to do than meet these people. It would be an adventure!

I was skeptical about any real work prospects developing from a cold, random audition such as this one. I felt jaded, verging on bitter, about "the business." The past year and a half had been an endless succession of career promises, none of them kept. First, I was told I'd get *this* movie. I didn't. Everybody was sure *that* sitcom would happen. They were wrong.

So when Garth Ancier, the legendary television programmer who basically started the Fox network and discovered the *Simpsons*, told his people to set up a meeting with me, I was like, "Yeah, yeah, sure—I've heard this one before." But I was in no position to turn my nose up at a job.

I didn't take the audition too seriously. I showed up at the Fox lot in my now rusty Honda, impressed by the gate and the guards and the logos stamped everywhere, but not wanting to get my hopes up since I'd been burned too many times before.

As I walked through the narrow streets of the mini-Hollywood metropolis on the way to the production office, I squinted at people riding in golf carts. These were people on their way to sound stages, people who had been chosen to entertain other people as I once had been. Until this moment, I hadn't realized how much I'd longed to be one of those people again.

I was now aware of how much this meant to me, but I tried to think of the meeting as nothing more than practice. I had fun. I spent two and a half hours flirting with three cute guys who, once I found myself working with them, turned out to be gay. (Big surprise, then, that they hired me, right?)

I signed my deal for *The Ricki Lake Show* at the age of twenty-three. Get ready, America: Downsized Ricki would be downsized no more.

⌒⌒⌒⌒⌒⌒

THE RICKI LAKE SHOW

That's what it said in big block letters on the carpet in the New York City TV studio where my talk show was taped. The moment when I first got a good look at that carpet remains one of the most significant and surreal of my career. I kept squinting, squatting, rubbing my eyes, taking it in from all different angles: *Had someone really woven my name into a carpet? Who had done this intricate needlework, and where did they live? Did they have any idea who I was? Was this whole thing some sort of cosmic joke?*

I mean, let's get real here. I was in no way qualified to be a talk show host appearing on national television five days per week. Once I got to know them, I found out that my producers had decided to audition me not on the recommendation of a director or an agent, but because they just happened to see me interviewed on someone else's talk show one slow news night. They thought I had a certain sparkle that might appeal to an audience no previous talk show host had been able to captivate.

I beat out more qualified candidates because the producers wanted this new show to be different from anything anyone had ever seen before. Instead of menopause, we would talk about men who—let's say—paused during orgasm. Okay, that's a made-up topic, but it wouldn't have been too weird or too risqué for my show. And our position on bad puns was: pro.

As a creative team, we were open to anything. I think it was precisely because I was enthusiastic, unstudied, and sort of naive that our formula worked from pretty much the first day we went on the air. We knew that people under thirty weren't interested in the rants of Donahue or Geraldo, but that they might take a moment to watch a host who spoke their language, whose frenetic style kept up with their thoughts—a host who asked genuine questions instead of leading ones, a host who provided laughs instead of hackneyed lectures on morality. Executives saw *The Ricki Lake Show* as a chance to capture a new daytime demographic.

And they were right.

Shortly after *Ricki Lake* started airing, the *New York Times* ran a profile on me. In trying to explain why I believed our show had become so successful in such a short period of time, I said, "Our show is funny. . . . It's not exploitative. It's not crude. It's not freaks. We're offering a clearer alternative to people who want to watch talk shows but feel they can't relate to the shows on menopause or whatever—the older skewing issues."

The profile went on to highlight all the ways in which I was different from the Jerry Springers and Sally Jessy Raphaels of the world. From the unique tactic I might use in order to grab the attention of a disrespectful guest—obviously pinch her on the leg—to which audience members I'd hand the microphone—nine times out of ten, if you're choosing between a cocky white guy and a confident black lady, she'll be the one with the more compelling comment—I wasn't afraid to do things differently. The truth is, I was just following my instincts, and I was lucky that, like so many times before, they led me in the right direction.

16

An audience could never buy me as
Brendan Fraser's love interest.

While the talk show was still in its infancy and toddlerhood, I kept my movie career going. I'd learned by now not to put all my eggs in one basket. After all, my first love was acting, and who knew how long this Oprah Jr. thing was going to last? I knew one thing for certain: I would never again find myself subletting another pool house because I was short on cash.

While the talk show provided pure, unadulterated nourishment for my ego, working in film still took a toll on my self-esteem—oddly, even more once I reached a healthy weight. As a chubby girl, I'd been a Hollywood curiosity, permitted to operate outside the rules of normal starletdom. Then, in 1996, I starred in a movie called *Mrs. Winterbourne*, along with Brendan Fraser and Shirley MacLaine. *Mrs. Winterbourne* was the first film in which I played a true ingenue—not the funny fat gal but the pretty object of desire, the straightforward romantic lead, the centerpiece of the movie. Although getting the role was a major victory for the cause of my self-esteem—theoretically, anyway—playing the role was anything but easy.

First, there was the matter of my wardrobe. Now you must be thinking, "You were thin by then, Ricki! Compared to the other films you had done, fittings for *Mrs. Winterbourne* were probably a walk in the park!"

Sigh. If only . . .

The person who put the clothes on my back, as well as on the backs of Shirley MacLaine and Brendan Fraser, was Theoni Aldredge, an accomplished award-winning costume designer who had worked on a slew of iconic Broadway productions, as well as a number of major films (*Network, Annie, Ghostbusters,* and *Moonstruck* among them). As I'm sure you can imagine, there's nothing an old-fashioned wardrobe mistress loves more than a human coat hanger, and no matter how thin I got, I could never become such a figure. Where someone like Theoni Aldredge craved angles, I offered nothing but curves.

Although I was working nonstop at being thin, I could never be thin enough for Theoni Aldredge. Trying to please her was an uphill, unwinnable battle, and I always felt that I was disappointing her, as though she were some parallel-universe mother figure who simply *wanted the best for me.* Where Divine had been my fantasy mother, Aldredge was my antimother. It's a cliché that the camera adds ten pounds, but it's true: all the people who look normal on film are not normal at all; they're skeletal. I was never skeletal. Add to that a closet full of unflattering, floral print granny dresses and it's no wonder I felt so discouraged, no matter how triumphant my weight loss. Making that film, I spent more time worrying about my weight than I did acting.

Once some really solid numbers came in for the talk show, I stopped moonlighting as an actress for a while. What a relief it was to know that I'd never again have to endure a humiliating costume fitting!

And all of a sudden I found myself with the time to fall in love.

I met Rob in New York while attending a Halloween wedding reception alone. I hadn't done much thinking about what I was going to wear to the festivities because I'd been rushed getting ready. The night before, I'd enjoyed a good old-fashioned one-night stand. So I wasn't really looking to impress anyone. I was just out to have a nice, low-key time, quietly basking in the glory of my recent sexual conquest.

The way I thought about and experienced sex had changed fundamentally since I'd lost weight and gotten my career back, but it was easy to forget anything had ever been wrong. I felt so confident about my body, so at ease in my own skin, that I took for granted that things hadn't always been that way.

I didn't even bother blow-drying my hair before leaving for the party. I jumped out of the shower, threw on a black CP Shades velour turtleneck and a long floral skirt—size 12—and ran out the door. As I caught a glimpse of myself in the mirror, I remember noticing that I had the dewy skin and natural flush that come only with sexual confidence and feeling really happy. I was still on the chunky side, but it didn't matter to me or any of the guys who flirted with me. Who knows why I was suddenly getting so much attention, but I suspect it had more to do with my attitude than the way I looked. Perhaps I radiated happiness. Perhaps I smelled of sex.

The moment I entered the party, Rob caught my eye from across the room. Dark and brooding, with boyish features and a mop of thick black hair, Rob approached me as soon as he noticed me looking at him. I could sense, the very second I met him, that I was going to marry him. I fell head over heels in love at first sight. I know, I know—I didn't used to believe in it either, but that was before it happened to me. From the moment Rob spoke to me, I could sense his exceptional intelligence and intense interest, and this combination turned me on.

Not to mention the fact that he was carrying a copy of Simone de Beauvoir's *The Mandarins,* an intense and difficult group biography about a group of French intellectuals at the end of World War II. I had no interest in reading such a book, but I had a keen interest in being with a man smart enough to be interested in reading such a book. Yes, looking back on it now, Rob's bourgeois bohemian persona seems a tad pretentious, but nothing could have been hotter to a twenty-five-year-old New Yorker in 1993.

Rob and I talked nonstop through the whole wedding reception, and by the end of the night, we had each told the other we were falling in love. I invited Rob to come home with me, but we didn't "do it," just made out tenderly for hours and fantasized about a future together. He left my apartment at 4:00 AM, and

I crumpled down against the door in a happy heap as it closed behind him.

The next day, he came back for our second date, bringing with him a bottle of red wine and a copy of Al Green's "Let's Stay Together."

We got engaged on our third date.

We got married in Las Vegas four months later.

I was very much aware of the way people must have perceived our relationship—as a rushed, adolescent whim. I was so worried, in fact, that our union would be dismissed as impulsive, that I was quoted in *People* magazine as saying, "We're not about getting attention. This is just the way it happened. It's so powerful. It just made sense."

In the same article, the reporter quotes my mother complaining that Rob and I were overly demonstrative of our affections for one another in public. "I think it's too much, if you want to know the truth," she said. Now that I'm a mom myself, I can see where she was coming from, admonishing us for pawing each other in a bowling alley, making our relationship fair game for a writer representing the country's highest-circulating gossip magazine. At the time, though, she just seemed like a buzzkill, envious of our youth and happiness. I remember my dad just sort of smiling innocuously in the background, waiting to see what would come next.

⚯

What came next were some really good years. Rob and I adored being together: lazing about in our small, sunny apartment downtown, shopping for books and records, grazing our way through the city's most delicious holes in the wall. We took rustic bike trips through the French countryside and relaxed on the beaches of Long Island. For the first year of our marriage, Rob and I lived in one big room, a studio loft apartment in the Village, and it was the only room we needed. I think it kept us together. It was so idyllic that even now that I have a home that could contain ten apartments just like it, I wish I had bought that one.

Rob was the first man who really helped me to unify my physical feelings and my emotional ones. I was comfortable enough with Rob to really *be* in my body, without needing to escape, in my mind, to anywhere else. Nothing about making love to Rob brought back memories of my childhood sexual trauma, and for a lovely, longish while, that was enough.

Turns out that the *People* gossip reporter was surprisingly insightful, though. Her profile on us as newlyweds had an eerily prophetic ending:

> "Our biggest issue is money," says Lake. "It's weird. My financial situation is so abnormal for someone who's 25, and for Rob, being a struggling artist, it's hard for him to compete with that. So we have to keep our heads straight and be secure with ourselves."
>
> "I'm sort of coming to terms with it," says Sussman, who will be bartending that night at a Village pub. "For a while, I was cranky about it, but this is going to be the deal from now on. I have to figure out a strategy for remaining sane.

She could support me, but that just seems really unhealthy and emasculating."

If only I had read that story a little more closely.

It's hard when both people in a marriage have self-motivated careers. Since both Rob and I were artists in a sense—I was a performer; he drew, painted, and contributed political cartoons to some really fine publications—neither one of us really had to answer to anyone but ourselves. Sure, I had an agent and producers keeping tabs on me, but everyone knew that I had a tendency to be harder on myself than anyone else could ever be. I was a desperately hard worker, and I didn't stop until I found success.

Rob, however, was more conflicted. Although his art was very important to him and he wanted to earn a living, he seemed to get stuck in his own way a lot more than I did. Even though his drawings were always exceptional and fascinating, he needed them to be perfect, and this perfectionism sometimes caused him to miss deadlines.

As his career lagged a bit, Rob settled into being a house husband. This would have been fine with me had he seemed fulfilled and emotionally available in this role—after all, I was earning enough for the both of us on my show—but he seemed disappointed in himself. Sometimes he'd be brimming over with frustration, sometimes he'd be subdued by what he perceived to be failure, but rarely was he the brilliant, dynamic man I'd fallen in love with anymore.

17

*I would never expect a baby
to save my marriage.*

By the time Rob and I had been married for almost four years, I was ready to have a baby. While I won't say I forced Rob into becoming a father sooner than he might have liked, I will admit that I wouldn't allow him to utter the words, "I'm not ready." Whenever I suspected that's where his mind was going, I'd playfully put my hand over his mouth or change the subject. I wanted a child more than anything else, and if we'd waited until Rob believed he was ready to be a father, we very well might be childless today.

Upon discovering that I was pregnant, I couldn't wait to tell my staff on *The Ricki Lake Show*. They had become like my family, so it's no surprise that they threw me a baby shower on my own show. Who knows why, but I was always pretty comfortable living my life in public, even before doing so became "a thing" that vaguely recognizable people are paid to do on random basic cable networks. (I'm talking about reality shows here—come on, you know you watch 'em.) Rather than seeing my audience's interest in my personal life as an invasion of my privacy, I felt honored to have the opportunity to introduce them to my husband, my children, and my friends. I wanted them to get to know me: Ricki the person, not the persona. I wanted to show them that I really was the girl I "played" on TV.

Maybe it's because I trusted my audience so explicitly that they trusted me too. In fans of *The Ricki Lake Show,* I connected with a massive group of people whom daytime broadcasters had never before tried to reach. These loyal viewers related intimately to me and my guests for eleven years—over the course of more than 2,100 episodes—and I think our interdependent dynamic was a precursor to today's reality TV. We all really felt that we knew each other. We became sort of the grown-up equivalents of imaginary friends.

The public enthusiasm on the news of my pregnancy touched my heart. There was nothing I wanted more than to manifest Rob's and my love for each other by creating a living being composed of equal parts of each of us while entirely its own person. Could I sound more like a hippie? Still, I mean every word of it. I think we both also hoped, like every other love-worn young couple on earth, that having a baby might make our marriage just a little bit easier.

18

*I'll never be able to accept my
body in its natural state.*

Something fundamental about my relationship to my body
changed when I got pregnant. I could feel this shift happening
almost immediately after Milo was conceived, even if it took me
much longer to articulate it.

Throughout my young life, I had seen my physical self as
an obstacle standing in the way of my happiness rather than as
a tool that could help me reach it. Because of my struggle with
weight, my body had always been something to work around,
not something that could work for me.

Every time I reached a new milestone during my pregnancy
with Milo, I marveled at the magic of it all. The human body's
miraculous tricks never ceased to amaze me. I guess I hadn't
necessarily trusted that my system would know what to do when

faced with this new predicament of housing and nourishing a living, breathing, tiny human—but it did. My body didn't betray me. It did right by me, and I was grateful.

Would you believe me if I told you that it was after a rapid weight gain of at least 40 pounds that I felt the best I'd ever felt about my body? That for the first time, despite pushing 200 pounds, I respected how my system worked naturally? That I was grateful for every cell, every inch, of my then undeniably abundant self?

That finally—at almost thirty years old—I found that I was no longer at war with my appetites but rather submitting wholeheartedly to them, letting my body's innate wisdom lead the way?

By carrying my two sons—Milo, who was born on March 22, 1997, and later Owen, who was born on June 18, 2001—inside my body for nine months, then shepherding them through the tunnels of my deepest self, and out into the world, I came to understand that my physical being was not a hindrance but a miracle: a vessel protecting and facilitating not only my own life but also these brand-new ones.

But at the same time I was flooded with the bliss of self-acceptance, I also mourned the loss of all the years I'd wasted hating my physical self as a funny fat girl. I had spent decades swallowing endless doses of criticism from without and within, letting poisonous junk food and vicious thoughts inflate my physical and emotional perimeters, hiding what I really looked like, as well as who I was inside. I had resigned myself to being the physical outcast, stuck forever on the sidelines of life.

I always felt somehow "less than" everybody else, even though, by definition, of course, I was "more than."

"Ricki Lake"—the persona, not the person—had always been the life of the party. She existed for the sake of everyone else's entertainment more than for her own self-actualization. In fact, it was the experience of charming and delighting others that she found most satisfying, because that is what she had trained herself to do, how she had learned to measure success, ever since she could remember.

I say *she* and not *I* because I am not that little girl anymore. Maybe I never really was her in the first place. Before I went through pregnancy and birth, taking on the responsibility of safeguarding a life other than my own, I didn't really know what it meant to be in control of my own destiny. I didn't understand that being a strong person means more than taking responsibility for yourself; it also means taking credit for what you accomplish.

Becoming a mother released me from the torment of an infinite self-criticism loop. It gave me the compassion to see myself as a child: a child who had listened to the grown-ups in her life, both real and imagined, for far too long.

I saw that I was capable of delivering myself from a life that wasn't making me happy by letting go of my childhood demons, my childhood persona, my material possessions, a great deal of weight, and, finally, my self-consciousness. But even after I got my show, married Rob, and became a mother, the transformation continued. As I honed my body, I used the wisdom I'd gleaned from the birth process to stay in touch with my spirit. In both childbirth and life—meaning, your own personal development—it's important to experience pain so you can go through it. We've come to refer to a struggle as "going through something" because this phrase implies forward movement rather than getting stuck in the dark. Too many of us, myself included, stay stagnant for too long because we're afraid to push through the pain.

The secret is learning to trust yourself, body and mind, and figuring out how to harness the power of your instinct and your intuition. A baby trusts that the scary dark tunnel through which it must travel on the way to its new life will lead to somewhere worthwhile. A baby knows when it has become too big to stay safely inside the womb.

A grown-up knows this too—when it is time to change old patterns and venture into uncharted territory. It's only when allowing yourself to experience the greatest pain that you will also know the greatest joy. Only through being truly present can we have an authentic birth experience, an authentic life. Only through deciding not to hide behind a fat suit—by unabashedly showing the world who we truly are—can we give birth to ourselves.

When Rob and I learned that we were pregnant with Milo, we wanted to do everything "right." I was young but my talk show gave me access to the best and the brightest doctors and health professionals all over the country, as well as a global platform on which to share what I had learned. I was happy to use my insider status "selfishly," in the best interests of my baby, and, I hoped, in the best interests of my viewers as well.

With my first pregnancy, Rob and I vowed to be as educated about the process and our options within it as was humanly possible. We steeped ourselves in the art and science of natural childbirth and came up with what we thought was a foolproof birth plan with which to welcome Milo into the world with as much love and comfort, and as little trauma and intervention, as possible. We decided to have Milo at a hospital with a "Birth Center," after meeting a friend of a friend who had just gone through a natural birth with the help of a midwife. Just three days after delivery, both mom and baby seemed blissful, not tired or traumatized. We decided we wanted the same amazing midwife to bring our baby into the world.

In order to deliver at the Birth Center, you had to commit to a drug-free birth. The Birth Center looked like a home, with a big bathtub in each room and all the emergency equipment hidden behind furniture and decor. The hospital looked, to me anyway, like a sterile place, for sick people.

There's an old Yiddish saying: "We make plans while God laughs." This sounds like something Grandma Sylvia would have said. Unfortunately, it describes all too well what ended up happening to our birth plan for Milo despite our months of careful preparation.

Milo's birth was nothing like we had expected. A few days before Milo's due date, the Virgo in me was getting restless. No matter when the little guy chose to show up, I had just six weeks of maternity leave before I had to go back to taping my show. I wanted to spend as much time as possible with my new baby.

Being a control freak, I tried natural remedies to jump-start my labor. I drank black cohosh tea and nothing happened. I took castor oil, which made me so sick I wanted to die. Stuff was shooting out from both ends of my body, but none of that stuff was a baby.

After twenty-four hours of nothing happening, Rob and I

went to the Birth Center to make sure everything was okay. My midwife wanted to go ahead with the delivery as we'd planned it, but because she had to follow hospital protocol, we were forced to move from the Birth Center to the traditional labor and delivery unit. This was obviously not our preference, but it was protocol, designed to prevent complications such as infection. It was off to the "hospital-hospital."

Pitocin was the first drug they gave me, to bring on my labor. A woman doesn't know how her body will respond to Pitocin until she tries it, and my body responded by going into camelback contractions—relentless, artificial contractions with no break between them. I started freaking out. In order to calm me down and take the edge off the pain, I was given Stadol, a mild painkiller. (I wanted to do everything I could to avoid an epidural.) This backfired, though, because the Stadol made me paranoid, and I became suspicious that something was wrong with my baby.

I was devastated. I couldn't help but feel as though my body had failed me—and that now, I was failing my baby. I tried to use the wise words of my friend, the doula Ana Paula Markel, as a mantra: *Labor is the struggle to find balance between control and surrender.*

In addition to my amazing midwife, I was supported by the OB/GYN on call, who went above and beyond her duties by getting on the floor underneath my hospital bed (a squatting position was much more comfortable for me than lying down), and making sure my baby was in a safe position. It was a different experience from what we had expected, but after thirty-six hours, Milo was born. When my mother came to visit me and Milo just after he was born and I introduced her to my midwife, I said, "Mom, here's the woman who delivered my baby!" My wonderful midwife corrected my statement immediately: "Ricki, *you* are the woman who delivered your baby. I helped you to deliver your baby."

Even though so many things had not gone according to plan, in the few precious moments when Milo was coming out of me, I was overwhelmed by a profound sense of bliss, self-acceptance, gratitude, and accomplishment that I had never experienced before. Even though the delivery had been very hard on both Milo and me, emotionally and physically, I knew immediately that giving birth to new life was what my body had been designed to do. And I knew that I wanted to help other pregnant women, no matter what their socioeconomic or personal situation, to discover the same thing.

Through a very difficult personal experience, I had discovered a much broader passion I would have never otherwise found. I vowed to learn as much as I could about the process of childbirth, for my own personal benefit and to help inform women with more limited access to information than I.

As Milo matured into an individual, I grew up a fair bit as well. When he was just five weeks old, I was walking by a holistic learning center in New York, when I noticed a pamphlet advertising an event called "The Art of Birthing." On a whim, I decided to check it out. The symposium blew my mind. It was supercrunchy; everyone wore Birkenstocks and long skirts, and people were knitting as they sat and listened to the lectures. Many of the women were nursing their newborns right there out in the open (the *really* talented ones were knitting at the same time). I was so impressed by the speakers at the event— experts who would later become my close friends—that I bought every book on the topic of birth. I knew that if I ever had to give birth again, I would do it differently. Everything about the birth movement fascinated me: the politics, the professions, the personal stories.

Long before I became pregnant with my younger son, Owen, I flirted with the idea of becoming a midwife myself one day. (I eventually decided that my talents were better leveraged as an advocate.)

When I learned that Rob and I had another baby on the way, just over three years after I had given birth to Milo, I knew how to explain virtually every detail of what I wanted when it came to our birth experience. I had been researching my options for a long time, and I felt confident that I would now be prepared for any situation. I would be able to safeguard myself—mind, body, and spirit—and that meant I could protect and nurture Baby Owen as well.

Just before we conceived Owen, Rob had planned a visit to China to see his best friend, who was temporarily living there. Rob really wanted to fly first class, and I pushed back, asking whether a ticket that cost thousands of dollars was really necessary when he was flying alone. After all, I was the one paying the bills. Ultimately I told him to take some time to think about it, then decide.

He decided, all right. To fly first class. Rob had a fabulous time in China, and he told me he thought this was because he had finally found his power. He really missed me while he was gone, he said, and he told me we could now have another baby. I hadn't planned on asking his permission to increase the size of our family, but I was glad he was on board.

All the birth world exploration I had done paid off when it was time to plan Owen's delivery. Making all the arrangements was empowering, even personally transformative. I was in charge of every decision that needed to be made, and that meant deciding who would be present for the birth, where I would choose to go into labor, and where I would actually deliver the baby. My options were no longer restrained by the information provided to me by the medical establishment or by the limitations they imposed on my own natural feminine potential.

At thirty-two years old, feeling confident that I understood all my options, I decided to give birth to Owen at home, in the bathtub of our downtown New York apartment. I hoped to find the most complete, transcendent experience I'd ever had—and I was not disappointed.

Owen's birth started out as anything but easy. I got to know every corner of our home as I paced back and forth all over it, treating my pain with movement, meditation, and pacing instead of narcotics. I found myself contemplating a question usually brought up by those opposed to natural birth: With all the advances in today's modern medicine, why would a woman choose to willingly inflict pain on herself? Even in that moment, when my body was preparing to endure agony, I was able to remind myself of the bigger picture. I came up with another way to look at it: Why would someone choose to put on blinders in order to shield herself from one of the most important experiences of her adult life?

The idea of experiencing pain on your own terms, in the service of something profound, is very empowering, no matter how much it hurts. Even at precisely the moments when you're feeling the worst pain, you can turn them into power. During those darkest times, it helps to remind yourself why you have chosen to go through something so difficult.

YOU ARE GETTING A BABY!

If ever I doubted that the way we humans come into the world has a profound effect on the person we become, Owen's serene little face and calm demeanor put an end to that. I think I gave my son an invaluable gift by delivering him in the most gentle way, in water. Even when he was just one second old, I could see the gratitude in his face. Almost immediately, he was alert, and calm, and connected to me. I believe that this special strength will stay with him, as well as unite us, forever.

Owen knows that his birthday is sort of my birthday as well. On some deep level, I think Owen understands how important the way he was born was—not just to his life but also to mine.

19

*I'll never feel my Grandma
Sylvia's presence again.*

An experience almost as transformative as giving birth to my boys was completing the three-day Avon Walk for Breast Cancer in 2000—the very day before I found out I was pregnant with Owen. In some sort of metaphysical way, doing that walk was almost like getting to meet my Grandma Sylvia as an adult, since breast cancer had been her own personal struggle, the villain that had stolen her from me. Now a grown woman, I was walking in her honor.

I don't think I've ever been as emotional as I was upon completing that walk. Because producers from my show were at the finish line to get footage of me crossing the home stretch, I have a tape of what we in the TV business call "B-roll" of these moments. B-roll consists of filmed background visuals that are used to support an interview or story. As an expert discusses an event on a news magazine program—say, the sinking of the *Titanic*—the producers cut away from the talking-head interview, and although you can still hear this person's voice explaining whatever he or she was talking about, you can see the thing itself illustrating their point. That's B-roll.

So catalogued in my home library of videos, nestled away with all the Letterman appearances and my kids' rock-and-roll recitals, is a tape of me finishing that breast cancer walk. Shot from what seems as if it must be hundreds of feet away from where I was standing, using a zoom lens, the scene is almost painfully intimate. All you can hear is the boom of music in the background, mixed up with the din of the massive crowd. I am unaware of the camera's location, so the whole thing has a voyeuristic quality.

I am wearing the same event T-shirt as everybody else at the walk, and it's big and unflattering. My hair is tucked up into a baseball cap, and I have no makeup on. Listening to the highly emotional music blasting over the massive loudspeakers and watching the legions of breast cancer survivors and supporters making their way across the finish line, I am sobbing uncontrollably for all the women around me—for their sadness and their strength. I am not only sobbing for the profound sense of powerlessness we all feel in the face of this terrifying disease, but also for the boundless sense of power we all feel when we band together as a united front to kick the shit out of it and support one another. I am sobbing because I can't wait to see my toddler, Milo, and his wonderful nanny, Marie.

I still remember how I felt that day, almost down to the cellular level: like such a tiny little being but proud to be a part of something so big. As cheesy as it may sound, it's moments like that that make me feel I can grasp the meaning of life just a bit.

Watching myself on the tape now, more than a decade later, I get emotional for a different reason. I see that those three days of walking tirelessly were a sort of meditation for me. The rhythm and continuity of my painful steps transported me back in time to being a sad little girl, devastated by the loss of the most important person in my life: Grandma Sylvia.

And as I made my way over the arduous route across the span of three days, sleeping fitfully in a tent on the ground, devouring beige slop under a rainy tarp, I was finally able to mourn the time Grandma Sylvia and I lost together. I imagined how much I would have loved to notice her lighthouse-bright grin out of the corner of my eye at all the important events in my life she had missed: the premiere of *Hairspray,* my wedding, the first taping of my show, the birth of my first baby. I was overwhelmed with anger by the fact that she had been stolen from me so young, but mostly I mourned the loss of all the moments we had never had.

Then I realized that I would never have made it to that moment without having—and *losing*—her.

After all the participants had crossed the finish line, the organizers asked me to step onstage and say a few words. I had trouble pulling myself together, but it was important to me to send my support and congratulations out to the incredible crowd.

"This is for Grandma Sylvia," was all I could really manage to get out.

And it was enough.

❦

Owen Tyler Sussman was born on June 18, 2001, at the beginning of one of the most beautiful New York summers I'd seen in a whole lifetime of living there. Owen was my New York baby. He seemed to embody everything I had always loved about the city: hope and energy, possibility and promise. And the way he was born, at home, in my bathtub, was idyllic. On maternity leave from my show, just after he was born, I relaxed in an oversized rocker positioned so I could gaze dreamily out the big, old windows of our cozy downtown apartment into the vastness of the Manhattan skyline, snuggling my tightly swaddled Owen and telling him all about the world. While I know it's impossible for life to be perfect, things at that time were pretty good.

Because the breast reduction I had undergone in my twenties had compromised my ability to nurse properly, I needed to supplement my breast milk with donor milk or formula. Supplementing involved strapping this crazy contraption around my neck, which made the milk squirt out from a tube located right in front of my nipple. All this rigmarole was to keep the baby from getting confused or frustrated while trying to latch on, since my own breasts couldn't produce enough milk to sustain him. But I wanted him to associate feeding with my breast, and not some cold plastic bottle, so the whole production was worth it.

One morning when I was sharing an intimate, nourishing moment with Owen and the contraption, I was struck by a strange news alert on the *Today* show.

"A small plane has hit the World Trade Center," reported a stunned Matt Lauer, who seemed as if he were playing one of those bit parts that anchors often portray in disaster movies.

"Rob!" I screamed toward the bedroom, where he was playing with Milo. "Come quick!"

The newscast continued. At that point, nobody had any idea what was happening. But from our kitchen windows we could see the towers and a lot of white smoke.

"Let's go up to the roof and take a look," Rob said, grabbing his camera and four-year-old Milo, who had asked whether he could come too. We didn't think for a moment not to let him, having no idea of what was going on out there.

We made our home in one of the tallest buildings in the West Village—it had nineteen floors—and so among all the three-story brownstones, it stood out. From the roof of our building, we had an unobstructed 360-degree view of the whole city, especially downtown to Wall Street. Standing up there on that platform in the sky provided us with the sense of being in the middle of the action while hovering somewhere outside reality.

Our little family stood up there half-dressed, huddled like refugees, watching smoke billow from Tower 1. Soon I noticed another plane heading in the same direction as the first. "THERE'S ANOTHER PLANE!" I shouted, and then I started screaming uncontrollably, producing primal sounds I didn't know my body could make. (They hadn't even come out during childbirth.)

Here I was at a point in my life where I felt that I was capable of conquering the world—I'd just given birth to a healthy baby in my own home; I'd found a new passion in the birth movement—and all of a sudden, it seemed that the world was going to end.

Those terrible moments were eerily silent. The scope of what was unfolding was so huge, the events so dramatic, that it felt as though we were watching a big-budget movie being shot on some sound stage that had been made to look like Manhattan. Except this was horribly real. As I looked over at Rob, who was capturing every horrible moment on film, I thought, *If I live through this terrible catastrophe, everything about my life is going to change.*

I kept screaming. I was sure those planes marked the end for all of us. I stared at the iconic peak of the Empire State Building, sure it was going to be next. I was so hysterical it hadn't occurred to me that my four-year-old child, standing next to me on the roof, was not likely to benefit from watching his normally stoic, in-control mother fall apart.

Rob grabbed me by the shoulders with both hands and shook me violently. "Your son is here!" he bellowed. I was grateful to him.

Rob did his best to calm me down, but it didn't work. I kept walking up and down from the roof to our apartment, pacing. I didn't know where to go.

That day I was surprised to learn that I am not the person you want to call in a crisis: I may seem strong, but I fall apart.

I felt like a failure for months because I hadn't been able to keep it together for my kid.

Subdued now, the three of us watched debris fall from the towers, floating down toward the ground at speeds that seemed at once to be both fast and slow. Of course, we didn't realize at the time that what we thought was debris was actually people jumping out of their office windows.

I am so grateful that our nanny, Marie, was there to help me take care of the boys. As always, Marie was the epitome of grace, soothing not only my children's nerves but also my husband's and my own. It was so painful for me to imagine that growing up in Africa, Marie had witnessed tragic moments like this one with horrifying regularity.

From our windows and our roof, we could see hordes of men and women covered in ash walking up Hudson Street like extras in a zombie movie. Our building was situated smack along the only direct route from the financial district to the Upper West Side, so anyone who managed to escape the chaos at Ground Zero walked right past our building.

Our neighborhood playground filled up with people lost in a daze of shock. We met John Waters there. He just happened to be in town from Baltimore, and we found comfort in each other.

We lost a lot of people that day, including the father of my son's best friend and a sweet twenty-nine-year-old firefighter who moonlighted working security on my television show.

I went back to work just two days after September 11. There was no way to deny that what we were producing was total dreck. Even though the city had been shaken to its foundations, we continued to take on the most insipid topics. I wanted to quit immediately. I no longer cared about baby-mamas or hoochiemamas, makeovers or make-unders. *Why am I here?* I asked myself. *Why am I not spending my time doing something worth-while? Life is too short.*

I was feeling totally disconnected from life. The only things that tethered me to some crumb of goodness in reality were my memories of the miracle of Owen's birth.

What do I want my legacy to be? I asked myself. All of a sudden, it mattered to me to *matter.* Everywhere I looked, high-profile people were lending their names to various causes, but I didn't want to jump on some bandwagon to help a cause that didn't need me just because I was feeling guilty about the state of the world. I wanted to find a cause that mattered—that would hold my interest and enable me to do good for the rest of my life.

As a result of this search for meaning, supporting the birthing rights movement became my passion. Even given what had happened on 9/11—*especially* given what had happened— I wanted as many women as possible to feel just as empowered as I had giving birth to Owen. I believed that every expectant mother deserved to feel powerful—in charge of the well-being of both her baby and herself. I wanted to work for all women to have the right to choose their best birth, regardless of birth setting, regardless of necessary intervention.

The birthing rights movement encourages a subtle yet profound sort of feminism. Being totally present through such an intense and rewarding physical experience shows a woman how strong she truly is. She expands her definition of what she is capable of.

I wanted that sense of mastery for women all over the world, and I wanted that for myself.

20

My husband and I will never
stop loving each other.

My marriage to Rob had begun to unravel even before we had the kids. While we had entered into our relationship as two young, creative individuals eager to see what each other would become, Rob was now stuck in low gear while my career picked up speed and my worldview grew broader and more complex. We didn't suffer any of the classic marital downfall issues: neither of us cheated, nor were we jealous, and there were no problems with physical attraction. I think competition, resentment, and envy were the roots of all our marriage's evils. As I grew up, we grew apart.

Rob had always struggled with mood swings, but the more successful I became, the more his ups and downs worsened. He went from being this whiz kid who pulsated with amazing potential—drawing witty cartoons, making gorgeous paintings, quoting difficult books—to being just a shell of his former self, shuffling around with barely enough energy to comb his hair.

Whereas once Rob had had a dashing swagger, now he seemed almost to walk with a limp. I was frustrated by his inability to bring his own creative projects to fruition because I truly believed he was a creative genius. I found it infuriating to see such talent go to waste, and it broke my heart to see this man I loved feeling unfulfilled.

I tried many times to help Rob find success, but it was clear that my mentoring him wasn't likely to have a positive effect on our marriage. My fear was that he'd start to see me as a nag, a mother figure, a goody-two-shoes older sibling, rather than his young and sexy wife. I could think of nothing I wanted less than to emasculate him, but I couldn't sit back in silence and watch his dreams of finding success as an artist fall apart.

Back when we were first married, Rob and I had decided to collaborate on writing and illustrating a children's book. Rob was excited about and grateful for the opportunity, overflowing with ideas about how to make it amazing, thrilled that he'd finally have a chance to make his mark.

I went to work at my talk show secure in the feeling that my husband would finally have a project of his own, something we could both be proud of. Sure, I'd lent my name in order to make the book deal happen, but I wanted it to be his baby. I wanted the world to get a peek inside his brilliant mind the way I had back when we'd fallen in love.

Twelve months after the day we'd been given the assignment and after spending hours upon hours in his studio, Rob wasn't finished. "It's just not ready yet," he told me.

More than a year after we'd signed the contract, still nothing. Once Rob came to terms with the fact that he wasn't able to do what he had promised, we had to give all the advance money back.

This didn't do much to improve my opinion of Rob as a life partner or boost his self-esteem. This cycle of disappointment continued through years and years of our marriage.

I knew that in order for Rob and me to move forward with our lives—whether we stayed together or not—something major needed to change. When I signed on for the eleventh season of my talk show, I decided it would be my last.

All of a sudden, I knew that our family should move from New York to Los Angeles in order to make a fresh start. It would be like going from a hospital birth to a home birth. I hoped we'd all be able to become more complete, fulfilled versions of ourselves there.

And although Rob, the boys, and I would make the move as a unit, I had a feeling we wouldn't be together for much longer.

21

*My husband could never become
someone I don't recognize.*

Rob didn't want to move to LA. To him, California was anathema
to who he was as a human being. LA was day; he was night. LA
was bright; he was dark. Life in LA was easy; Rob liked things
hard. All the reasons Rob rejected California were the reasons
I knew I would love it. I was certain that moving west would
give the boys and me a chance to emerge from underneath the
dark cloud of Rob's moods—sad swings that might have been
the fault of his brain chemistry rather than his character but
that hurt us deeply nonetheless.

As Rob and I drifted apart emotionally, toward the very
end of our marriage, our physical connection began to fall away
as well. The sex was the last thing to go. Losing our physical

chemistry saddened both of us deeply. That part of our lives together had always been effortless.

For me, it brought up many questions. Now that my relationship with the most important man in my life was ending,
how would I feel about my body? Would I be propelled back into
the insecurities that plagued me during my teen years? I had
put on some weight since becoming a mother, that was for sure.
Would I again feel vulnerable to the stares and touches of others, the way I had when I was little? Would remembering Joe,
Mario, Aidan—and now my failed marriage—cause me to hide
by putting on weight?

I hoped not, and deep down, I didn't think so. Leaving my
marriage to Rob as a soon-to-be-single woman, I sensed that my
best days were yet to come.

Although my marriage to Rob had been falling apart for
what seemed like forever, by the time Owen became a toddler,
the tension was too much for me to bear.

And by that time, we had moved to LA. During my frantic travels back and forth from coast to coast (I was still completing the final season of my show), I had managed to see and
fall in love with a sprawling, old-fashioned house in the Brentwood section of Los Angeles, nestled high in the hills, just a few
miles from the ocean. The house had belonged to the actress
Courteney Cox, whose impeccable taste made it feel like home,
even before we moved in. Having learned what it feels like to
lose a home to foreclosure, I paid for the Brentwood house in
cash, so that no matter what happened, nobody would be able to
take it away from me.

As soon as the sale closed, I set to work making the

Brentwood house a haven for my boys. We would be moving from a 2,100-square-foot apartment—huge in New York—to a 7,000-square-foot house in Brentwood—huge anywhere. The new house had beautiful grounds and a magical swimming pool. When I was a little girl on plane rides, I used to count swimming pools from the sky, always dreaming I'd have my own one day—and now I did.

Now I had the idyllic suburban landscape in which to give my growing boys a happy childhood. I had two little boys who would grow accustomed to wearing shorts in winter and running barefoot whenever possible. I was happy to trade my black sweaters and boots for loose linens and flip-flops.

Just a couple months on the left coast, and we already looked like a perfect California family—except Rob had left his heart in New York. As we figured out our new life in California, it became clear that our marriage wasn't going to survive the move. After many gut-wrenching conversations, Rob and I finally decided to divorce. We didn't want our children to one day emulate what had become a dead relationship.

It has been very difficult for me to decide to share this very personal part of my story. Now, almost ten years after splitting up, Rob and I have managed to stay pretty good friends, and we treasure the opportunity to co-parent our boys without getting mired in our personal problems. As a father, Rob has been a constant presence in my boys' lives, and they worship him. I would never choose to reveal anything that would violate his privacy or make my children question the bonds holding their family unit together. Divorce has become sort of a taboo subject in our culture, because of all the icky personal discussions that come with it—money, intimacy, and anger among them. That said, if I can in any way provide emotional support or tactical knowledge to other women facing divorce, I feel it's my responsibility to do so.

Once Rob and I agreed to divorce, the matter was no longer personal. Our attorneys were running the show. For some reason, both our attorneys wanted to serve the other party first, so Rob and I entered into a game of cat and mouse. I brought the boys along on a work trip to New York, where I was starting what would be the final season of my show.

One gorgeous afternoon, my good friend Frances and I took our kids out for pizza in the Meatpacking District. All of us were happy to be back on the East Coast after spending time in LA.

As we walked past SoHo House, a private social club I belonged to at the time, I was stopped in my tracks by a young woman whom I assumed was a fan.

"Are you Ricki Lake?" she asked.

"Yes!" I said, with the warmth I genuinely feel toward those who appreciate my work.

"I'm sorry, but I have to serve you," she said, handing me divorce papers. My face went white. It was humiliating.

Because Rob and I decided to split up, even though we'd just moved our life out to Los Angeles, we had to relocate temporarily back to New York. The last season of my show would be filmed there, and with our family in a state of turmoil, Rob and I wanted the boys to be physically close to both of us as much as possible. The last thing either of us wanted was for Milo or Owen to feel abandoned by either one of us—it was our marriage that was failing, not our family.

Since we had already bought our Brentwood house and sold our New York apartment, we had to find new temporary apartments for our return to New York. We rented three places—one for Rob, one for me and the boys, and one next door, for our nanny Marie. The boys quickly became accustomed to the ins and outs of joint custody, shuttling back and forth between these new places. I was heartbroken for them, but they were amazingly resilient. Both Rob and I were really proud.

Soon after we moved back to New York, Rob and I met at a coffee shop on 16th Street to talk about the terms of our split. I was beyond nervous about what I had come to this meeting to do: present my soon-to-be ex-husband with what I considered to be a generous offer so that we could settle our divorce out of court and co-parent effectively, as friends. Although we had a prenuptial agreement that entitled Rob to absolutely nothing, should we separate, I made him an offer that would enable him to take care of himself and the boys in the sort of environment and lifestyle to which we'd all become accustomed. Remember that I had been supporting our family from Day One. Rob had earned nary a penny.

As I waited to hear his thank you, Rob told me that the offer was unacceptable. Half of me wanted to yell and scream my head off; half of me wanted to slip down under the table, and sob quietly. I tried to respond with as little heated emotion as possible. If I'd had any doubts about the divorce, they had vanished now.

As much as I have yearned for more supportive parents, I have been blessed throughout my life by other role models and care-givers who have always had my back. The one I am most in-debted to is my longtime business manager, Howard. Howard has the brain of a rocket scientist and the foresight of a fortune-teller, and before I married Rob, he insisted we sign a strict pre-nuptial agreement highlighting the assets we each had before the marriage (none), and protecting the future proceeds of our careers. It essentially stated that neither of us was entitled to the future earnings of the other.

Remember that back when we were young, Rob had been a promising artist and musician. There was no reason to believe that he wouldn't be a wild financial success on his own, and if he was, I agreed to claim no part of his earnings should we go our separate ways. By signing the prenup, he made the same promise to me. We were both madly in love with each other for all the right reasons, and this antimaterialistic gesture proved it.

Flash-forward ten years: Rob got bad advice when his law-yers encouraged him to challenge this prenup, because nobody is smarter than Howard and Howard's prenups are iron-clad.

No matter how you've come to feel about the relationship, it is utter torture to have to bear constant witness to the messy, heartbreaking dissolution of the most important romantic re-lationship in your life. You have to get used to people—people you know and people you don't—all over the world seeing you be painted as a villain, with no way to salvage their opinions of you. You worry that you might lose all the money you've worked so hard to earn. You agonize over the custody of your children, the two most important human beings who have ever existed in your world.

You remember what your world was like before everything fell apart.

Having to be in court constantly was a nightmare, but I'll admit that the bizarre cast of characters surrounding us there made it just the teeniest, tiniest bit entertaining. Showing up for my divorce proceedings felt like guest-starring on *Night Court*.

First, there was the bailiff, a mountain of a man who smiled at me whenever he could and left me handwritten poetry and Nordstrom gift cards taped under the table where I sat each day. There was my brilliant, yet occasionally inappropriate lawyer, who made me drive to his home every morning so we could travel to court together—"a united front"—in his Jaguar. There was the judge, who weighed at least 350 pounds and was famous for screaming so violently at unprepared lawyers that they ran right out of his courtroom.

Allow me to let you in on a little secret: All the people in the divorce business are friends. What goes on in that courtroom is a bunch of theatrics. Once you're able to see the machinations, all the "drama" becomes as exhilarating as discovering what's behind the curtain in *The Wizard of Oz*. If I hadn't been busy trying not to lose everything important to me in my life, I would have pitched a reality show.

A prenup is considered invalid until proven valid, and even if you're in the right, you don't get back the money you spend on legal fees trying to validate it. After a year of expensive legal fees, my prenup had held up. But I had spent more than seven figures worth of my hard-earned cash to protect what was mine in the first place. If I can offer any unsolicited advice to people going through the trauma of divorce, I'll do it in one word: mediate (settle out of court).

When Rob and I were working out the initial custody arrangements, my schedule was brutal. My show still filmed in New York, but our family was in the process of re-relocating to Brentwood, so when I wasn't on camera, I was on an airplane.

Every other weekend, when the boys were with their dad, per our custody agreement, I would leave New York to spend the weekend in LA. I wanted to get acclimated and supervise construction on the new house renovations, but I was also itching for some grown-up time—the opportunity to let my hair down. Ours had been the divorce from hell, and I was in desperate need of an escape. "Do you know anyone that would like me?" I asked a friend of mine. I needed some attention. "Yes!" my friend replied. "His name is Anthony, he's a personal trainer, and he is hot." Just what the doctor ordered.

Before I knew it Anthony and I were sleeping together. His presence—and stamina!—made my weekend visits to LA satisfying on all levels. Although the commute was brutal, all that racing from coast to coast was worth it.

My typical schedule was this: I would tape my show until

around six at night, then jump into the car, leaving myself in the hands of my genius driver, who used to be a New York cop. He would race me to JFK Airport, weaving in and out of lanes on the Long Island Expressway, in order to make sure my ass was on the last American Airlines flight to Los Angeles.

Arriving at JFK, I'd hightail it to the gate, collapse into my first-class seat, and take an Ambien. I'd get five hours of sleep and wake up when I arrived in LA, where it was only ten o'clock at night because of the time difference.

Anthony and I would stay up half the night running around LA doing fun things and the other half fucking each other. Come Sunday night, having slept nary a wink, I would drag myself onto the red-eye, the last Sunday night flight out of LA back to New York. Immediately I would take my Ambien, get a few hours of sleep, and return to my talk show set. I maintained this crazy schedule every other week for six months as we finished taping my show's last season.

While my relationship with Anthony was by no means casual, I wasn't ready to get seriously involved—I was still emerging from a ten-year marriage. I was suffering too much over all the worry, and I lacked the necessary brain and heart space to begin a real relationship.

22

Our family will never be the same again.

———

The next few months were hard. Getting used to the new normal of being a single parent is totally surreal, even if your marriage has been in shambles for a long time. Besides the pervasive sense of personal failure I beat myself up over pretty much constantly, I had to get used to our bizarre new living situation.

California divorce laws have a provision for the protection of young children called "bird nesting." Instead of shuttling the kids back and forth between parents' homes at the beginning of a shared custody arrangement, it's the parents who move from house to house.

This is a smart idea, really: it provides children with a basic sense of consistency during a volatile time, and it gives parents a break from their familiar domestic space. But it's hard when you're traveling back and forth from New York to California at least twice a month to film your talk show, even though you "live" in LA. I got pretty discombobulated shuffling from my Brentwood house, to the Luxe Hotel down the street, to a hotel in New York. I felt like a vagabond.

Thank God, it didn't take long before my commitment to my show was finished—eleven seasons and 2,100 episodes complete!—and I was living in LA full time. Rob rented a big old house in Beverly Hills, next door to Pia Zadora, that the boys loved. Marie, who was basically their second mom (and remains so to this day), made traveling from place to place as easy on them as possible. She actually managed to fill their chaotic lives with pure childhood joy.

I continued my relationship with Anthony and although I knew I wouldn't stay with him forever, he was perfect company at the time, providing me with love, compassion, and physical pleasure, without commitment pressure under which I would have collapsed. We took some great trips together—going to Machu Picchu and South Africa—and he enjoyed spending time with my kids. They got a kick out of seeing me happy.

Once I finally reestablished a stable home life for my sons, it was time for me to embark on manifesting my dream project. I was ready.

23

I'll never do anything really important.

After all the details of my divorce were finally settled, I forced myself to take a deep breath and contemplate an intense existential question: Besides my two incredible children, what did I want to leave behind as my legacy?

After more than twenty years' worth of striving for approval, finding it, then discovering it wasn't enough to satisfy me, I decided to make a documentary about the subject that was truly closest to my heart: giving birth in America.

In delivering my two boys, I had come to see that giving birth could make many women feel powerless, and disconnected from their physical selves. This seemed totally backward to me, and it broke my heart. But I understood. Even though it had ended with a miracle—Milo!—my experience delivering Baby Number One had not gone according to plan, and part of me felt like a failure. But instead of surrendering to the status quo, I used my disappointments with my first time around to fuel an investigation of all that was possible when it came time for my second.

All my inquiry had paid off when I delivered Owen in my bathtub at home. I remembered how giving birth to him had freed me from many of the struggles I'd long endured with my own body. It even seemed to help heal wounds I'd long believed were gangrenous—the horrific memories of sexual abuse I'd suffered as a child. Giving birth had finally returned ownership of my *own* body to me.

I wanted every pregnant woman to have the chance to experience what I had: the pure magic of the natural human birth process. I had come to believe this experience was the key to a woman's being able to integrate her spiritual, physical, and psychological selves.

I had filmed the experience of Owen's home birth, but I never really knew what I was going to do with the footage. Three years after he was born, I got the idea of sharing the footage with expectant women who were considering giving birth at home in order to demystify—and I hoped, destigmatize—the process. Although I didn't feel beautiful in the video, I knew that it depicted a beautiful, rarely seen moment. And the cause trumped my vanity in this case.

I needed to bat the idea around, but there were only a handful of people in the world with whom I'd feel comfortable sharing a tape of me naked in a bathtub and only a handful of this handful were in "the business." But I was sure I had a really big idea—my biggest yet—and I needed a partner to help make my dream a reality.

I met Abby Epstein when she directed me in an off-Broadway production of Eve Ensler's hit play, *The Vagina Monologues.* Pretty amazing coincidence, considering our next collaboration would also be all about vaginas!

At the point when we started the project, I was a mother, while Abby was not. Abby was a well-known theater director in New York, having directed many of my favorite plays, from *Rent* to *Hedwig and the Angry Inch.* She had just finished directing *Until the Violence Stops,* a documentary about the playwright Eve Ensler's crusade to end violence toward women and girls.

Rather than start a conversation about home birth with Abby, risking the possibility that she might not relate, given the stage where she was in her own life, I showed her my home video. To my relief, as we watched it, Abby was rapt—speechless with amazement. She told me that she had always associated the act of giving birth with stark, white hospitals, with pain, with blood—and that this was so much the opposite, it seemed almost to come from another world.

"We have to get people to see this!" she said, and I smiled, knowing I had found the right collaborator. When I rattled off some statistics to Abby—that home-birth rates had declined from 95 percent in 1900 to less than 1 percent by 1955—she told me that she saw the universal theme of this story as being about a woman's control over her own body and, by extension, her own life. This wasn't just a women's rights project; it was a human rights project. Abby and I set out to make a documentary that would give women all over the world access to the knowledge I had worked so hard to find.

Once Abby and I had put together a proposal for the project, we thought backers would be clamoring to finance it. The only difficulty we'd have would be choosing among our many cinematic suitors.

Boy, were we wrong.

Everywhere we went, producers were concerned that our idea was too graphic, too fringe, too hippie, too left, too feminist, too backward, too modern. To make a long story short, everybody was afraid of our movie.

But the bottom line is that there is no human being on this planet who hasn't participated in the birth process at least once. And because of that fact, we knew the film would have broad appeal. We decided to proceed on our own, with my post–*Ricki Lake Show* nest egg paying production costs until we could sell our finished film on the back end.

We traveled all over the world interviewing doctors and midwives, mothers and fathers. We found a hospital in Brazil where over 90 percent of babies are delivered by C-section and where the waiting room has a piano bar. The joke down there is that the only women who give birth vaginally are those whose doctors get stuck in traffic.

We met glamorous celebrities who felt glamour had no place in their child's birth and who sweated out their labor in the company of friends and family at home.

We got to know every player in the birthing business in

New York, finding intelligent and experienced experts to speak on every side of the issue.

And Abby even got pregnant. We filmed every step of her birth journey, which, despite being planned as a home birth, eventually resulted in an emergency hospital C-section that delivered preemie Matteo five weeks early (he is now a healthy and happy five-year-old). Although Abby's difficulties delivering Matteo are heartbreaking to watch; they are key to the success of the film. We aimed to present the broad range of options and the even broader range of realities of giving birth without censoring anything—even ourselves.

When *The Business of Being Born* was finally finished, we had no trouble finding backers to distribute it. It premiered at the Tribeca Film Festival in 2007 to humbling acclaim.

We traveled around the world showing our film, facilitating discussions about childbirth choices, and standing up for midwives and doulas and moms who'd never before had a public voice. We wanted to bust open the world of obstetrics, exposing all the injustices and misinformation that American women had been forced to tolerate for far too long.

First-wave feminism had positioned motherhood as something that limited a woman's capacity for social power, but we saw things differently. Abby and I believed a woman could harness her most profound strengths through the birth process, but only if she became an active participant rather than a passive patient blindly following the path doctors had mapped out for her.

Now that I was becoming an advocate for childbirth choices, I could imagine my life holding meaning for people beyond those in my own intimate orbit. Entering the world of birth didn't feel like working; it felt like living.

24

I'll never waste time on the superficial again!

When it came time to do publicity for *The Business of Being Born*, I knew I had to make a big splash. While I was sure America would be eager for the information presented in our film, I knew it would be difficult to get people into movie theaters to watch some earthy-crunchy-feminist diatribe. Of course, that's not what our film was at all, but there was no denying certain associations people were bound to make before they saw it.

I saw part of my mission to be changing the face of childbirth choices. I wanted to prove that having a baby at home and being a glamorous modern woman were not mutually exclusive. I wanted to make a real splash when I took the film around to show it off. So what did that mean? Looking absolutely incredible. And this meant getting really, really thin.

I'm the first to admit I am a bundle of contradictions.

I know that whittling away my excess flesh to achieve a Holly-wood level of perfection in the service of presenting a documentary about letting women's bodies do their natural thang sounds a bit hypocritical.

But I am also a twenty-year veteran of the news media machine, and I know what makes a good story. I wasn't going to let this film languish and die on the dusty shelves of health food stores just because I didn't look a certain way. I didn't want to give mainstream America even one excuse to ignore what we had gone to great lengths to show them.

When Howard Bragman, my publicist at the time, and I found out that the film had been accepted to premiere at the Tribeca Film Festival, arguably the highest-profile event on New York's movie scene, we decided I needed to look my best. And "looking my best" meant going on a diet.

Now a lot of "experts" claim that the keys to "effortless" weight loss are lifestyle choices, emotional closure, regular exercise—and certainly these are all important. But in order to lose weight, you need to eat less, plain and simple. Shifts in habit and outlook are key, but if you want your body to make a big change, you've gotta send it a serious memo.

Although I was by no means heavy when we finished the film, I had kind of been lying low when it came to my appearance. I just hadn't had the time or the focus to get my body into tip-top shape when we were in the heat of working on the documentary. Now that we were getting ready to present it, though, I had to get ready to present myself.

I began right after January 1, the time of year every single American citizen is constitutionally required to start a new diet.

I wanted to be sure I was successful, in a big—then small—way, so I assembled a team of experts.

In order to be able to control every morsel I put in my mouth for the next nine weeks, I signed up for a meal delivery plan that called for a $5,500 check upfront. If I was paying $5,500 for a diet, you could bet I'd be sticking to it.

I took a deep breath and promised myself that if I didn't overthink things and just ate what I was given, this plan would work. And it did.

I lost thirty-five pounds in nine weeks, the fastest drop I'd ever seen in all my years of dieting. The change was so fast that it almost seemed to happen overnight, and a new, sexy shape to my body emerged that I had never seen before.

While I think it's utterly ridiculous when people say things like, "Eighty percent of weight loss is mental!" it's true that you have to channel a certain mind-set to "release" weight. You have to believe it will happen. Getting ready for the premiere, I promised myself a total transformation, and I got one. It was the second time I'd gotten the itch of a caterpillar ready to turn into a butterfly, and I just went with it, silencing any negative thoughts inside my head.

There was something similar in the way my body transformed before the release of the film, and before I gave birth to my boys. In both situations, I sat back and let my physical self take control. I trusted that my body would do what it was supposed to. This wasn't a case of its obeying me or vice versa, but of my body and mind coexisting in natural homeostasis.

25

*I'll never feel comfortable
being photographed.*

⁓

I don't know that I've ever had as much fun as I did on the press
tour for the premiere of *The Business of Being Born*. It was a
whirlwind of red carpets and screenings, morning show appearances, and moments of intense connection with total strangers.
During those couple of months, I was probably photographed
more frequently than I had ever been in my life, and I almost always look happy. Before you think I'm the shallowest person in
America, let me tell you that this happiness was just 10 percent
due to the fact that I was the thinnest I'd ever been and 90 percent because I felt like I was really changing the world my own
teeny bit.

In addition to star-studded events such as the Tribeca Film
Festival, we showed our film all over the country in small the-

aters, to communities of midwives, doulas, pregnant women, and progressive health professionals. It was impossible not to get emotional during the Q&A sessions after these showings, as I looked out at the faces of women and children who were eager to help our country rethink the way we give birth. There were homemade cards and carrot cakes, beaming babies and humble husbands (and partners and wives). It was as if all these people who had been invisible were coming out of the woodwork to see our film, using it as a reason to announce their presence to the world. I could really feel a groundswell, and I was beyond proud to be a part of it.

Not every moment was a carrot cake walk, however. Some difficult experiences took me by surprise and made me dizzy with the fear of being misunderstood. Probably the most difficult was when we screened the film for some of the people closest to my heart: the doctors, nurses, and midwives of the New York City hospital where I'd delivered Milo.

We were beyond excited to screen our film in the setting where we'd shot a good portion of it. The staff and patients had been totally accommodating in giving us an all-access pass to their OB/GYN unit, letting us capture moments both triumphant and troubling.

And of course I would be forever grateful to the hospital for making my delivery of Milo successful despite its complications. My doctor, who happened to be on call when Milo's birth became an emergency situation, had been my unqualified hero. She arranged for me to have what is called a "walking epidural," which is pain medicine that doesn't paralyze the mother, so I could be as active as possible during the delivery. When I needed to squat instead of lie flat on my back, she got under my hospital bed in order to see the position of the baby's head, acting as if it was no big deal so I wouldn't be uncomfortable. I would be forever grateful to her for how beautifully she'd handled Milo's delivery, and I couldn't wait for her to see *The Business of Being Born.*

Watching the movie in that hospital screening room, there were more than a few times Abby and I shot each other nervous glances. I don't think I'd really understood until that moment how the hospital professionals might have felt criticized by the way the film portrayed them. Unfortunately, our cameras had been privy to more than one instance when unnecessary interventions had been taken and some of the young doctors at times seemed insensitive. In no way did I regret the hospital scenes we had shown, but I was nervous to see how the staff would receive them.

After the screening, I couldn't wait to catch up with the doctor who had delivered Milo, to get her thoughts on the film and an update on her life. I saw her across the room when the lights came on and rushed to give her a warm hello. All I got in response was a cold, steely acknowledgment as she told me she was furious about the way her hospital came across in the film. The post-screening Q & A session was heated. One hospital official called us "irresponsible filmmakers." We were aghast. This was a heartbreaking moment for me, not only because important personal relationships had suffered, but also because I was witnessing the all-or-nothing polarization this issue could bring out in otherwise reasonable people.

There was no question that the film Abby and I had made had a strong point of view. While we made an effort to show both sides, we felt that the birthing rights movement was strongly underrepresented in the media, and we were proud to stand up for it.

26

I'll never be in a serious relationship again.

⌒〰〰〰

Finally arriving back in LA after what had been an emotional roller coaster of a press tour, I was happy to settle into my regular Brentwood life again. I truly relished taking my kids to school, music lessons, and sports; playing with my dog in our backyard and swimming pool; hosting piano sing-alongs featuring my talented friends; taking hikes in the majestic mountains high above our neighborhood.

Anthony and I continued dating. He wanted things between us to grow more serious. It frustrated Anthony to no end that I never invited him to move into the big Brentwood house to live with me and the boys; after all, we spent most nights together, and he even came along on our family vacations.

But I didn't ask Anthony to move in because deep down, I knew I could never move forward with him. We just weren't a couple who could last forever, and if there was no chance of forever, I wasn't going to risk interrupting my boys' routine, putting their happiness and security on the line again, if I knew things wouldn't work out.

I was still overwhelmed with tremendous guilt about the failure of my marriage to Rob. I had made a commitment, and I had broken it. After having babies with Rob, I made the choice to leave him, ended our marriage, and put our boys through hell. There was no question that when I agreed to marry Rob, I believed we would last forever. I had been wrong, and I was more than a little bit angry at myself for that. I wasn't going to make the same mistake twice.

Anthony stuck around a lot longer than he probably should have. He resented my inability to commit to our relationship, and rightfully so. He was right to want to be my partner after being such a consistent presence in our lives. He was in his mid-thirties and ready to settle down, and I couldn't give him what he wanted. We were coming from very different points of view: I thought it was a big deal when I gave him two shelves in my closet. After two and a half years of being together, giving him those shelves was a serious slap in the face for him.

The beginning of the end with Anthony came when Abby delivered her baby. Anthony and I had had a petty argument the day before, and he was holding a grudge. When Abby's water broke, five weeks before her due date, I raced immediately to her side in New York. I was her doula, having pledged to help her through her labor.

It angered Anthony that I was rushing to Abby's side, even though he knew she was like a sister to me—Abby and I had been making our film for most of the time he and I had been dating. Not only did he not offer to come with me to see Abby in New York, he didn't even ask how she was doing, or offer any words of support. He was so insecure about his position in my life that he couldn't bear to see someone else take priority.

When I returned to Los Angeles, despite the fact that Anthony and I had drifted apart emotionally, Anthony and I continued to be physically intimate. We really loved each other on some level, and it was almost impossible to separate, even though we both knew it was inevitable. Needless to say, in the late stages of our relationship, my mind started to wander.

Remember how, during my divorce commute, I got used to falling asleep on Ambien?

Ambien is no joke. Although it seems as though everybody I know has a prescription for it, it's really, really powerful. While nothing beats it as a fast-acting sleep aid, Ambien is notorious for producing some pretty insane side effects. People experience short-term memory loss, as well as temporary amnesia. I suffered both of these at some point or another, but I chalked up my wackiness to stress. As far as I knew, Ambien was a perfectly safe little pill that helped me get the rest I needed.

I would like to propose adding the following warning to the literature that accompanies an Ambien prescription: *Do not take this pill until you are ready to go to sleep.* Once you've chased that baby down with a glass of water, you'd better be ready for your head to hit the pillow. Because if you force yourself to stay awake through Ambien's initial tiredness-inducing period, you're in for a wild ride—one that you may or may not remember.

I need to preface the following story by emphasizing that I am not a cheater. I've never cheated on anyone, never even entertained the thought. Leaving my marriage was never about meeting someone else; it was only about being alone.

One night during my relationship with Anthony, I downed my Ambien, then decided I wasn't really ready to go to bed yet. I was bored, so I figured I'd play around on the computer.

"You know what would be fun, Ricki?" mused my Ambien-crazed self, "signing up for online dating!" My first destination, eHarmony, was the vaguely conservative dating website with creepy commercials starring an old "doctor" guy who claims to know what's best for you. Yeah, not really the most appropriate online home for a famous liberal person with an on-again, off-again boyfriend. But stoned on prescription sleep aids, I couldn't resist the temptation to provide my credit card number and fill out an endless number of forms. *I love personality tests! My favorite book is* The Kite Runner! *I'm looking for a man who can support himself! Got any more personality tests?*

I finally fell asleep and forgot all about it.

The next day, I started receiving all these e-mails with the subject line, "Match Found!" and I was like, *What crazy spam. Deleting, deleting, deleting. Weird!* I had no recollection of where any of these messages could be coming from. None.

I might have never discovered their origin had Anthony not been using my computer one day to check his eBay listings.

He was browsing around in Safari, and the eHarmony shortcut came up on my computer. I was literally looking over his shoulder as he navigated—waiting to see whatever eBay item he was dying to show me—and with a funny expression on his face, his pointer hovering over the eHarmony shortcut, Anthony asked me, "What's this?"

"I don't know, what's that?" I asked. Thinking, *We're playing a game, maybe? I certainly have no idea. I'll play along.*

Anthony clicked on the shortcut, finding my eHarmony profile.

At first, I drew a blank—*What the hell is that?*—but then it all started coming back to me in fragments, the way it feels when you're remembering a dream. Once my mind had assembled enough information to form a crude recollection, I found myself saying, "Oh, wait a minute, yeah, that does sound familiar."

Anthony stormed out of the room despite my protestations and apologies. I was laughing hysterically: "I swear, baby, I didn't mean to do it!" But he was hurt nonetheless. The whole shenanigan put some serious distance between us. Our relationship, even the purely physical part, was never the same again.

To this very day, Anthony believes that I was cheating on him with the help of a conservative Christian website. He thinks I was seriously exploring my options when what I was was delirious on Ambien. It's a funny story, with a sad ending: Anthony never forgave me. He never trusted me again.

So now I was *really* single. What was I supposed to do? Go back online? I *had* already broken the seal.

And so began my (mis)adventures in online dating . . .

27

I'll never be irresponsible.

Each night after my boys had gone to bed, I cozied up to my laptop with a glass of wine or a bottle of bubbly water and prepared to do some online shopping. For men.

The way I saw it, in order to preserve my sanity, I had to balance all the serious political and intellectual work I was doing on behalf of *The Business of Being Born* with some good, old-fashioned fun on the Internet. So maybe I was acting out a little bit. At the time, I was looking for a cheap thrill, and since I'm a good Jewish girl from Westchester—a mother!—neither heroin nor skydiving was an option.

eHarmony was just the tip of the iceberg. Now I was ready to branch out. With the eHarmony gaffe, I'd been forced to do the time without doing the crime. There was nothing I could do to make Anthony believe I truly hadn't cheated on him. So why the hell not keep going? I was lonely, and I figured now was as good a time as any to become an expert at being courted over the Internet.

I doubt I would have been putting myself out there had I not felt so ridiculously confident about my body. I'd taken a couple weeks off *The Business of Being Born* promotion train to do a Lifetime movie in Canada in which I played a single career woman who finds out she has breast cancer. While we were shooting, I picked up some kind of stomach bug and got really, really sick—so sick that I had to be admitted to the hospital for IV rehydration. Although I could barely keep gelatin down, I was overjoyed to find out that I weighed only 120 pounds. This was the tiniest I'd been since sixth grade! I believed that being so small made me entitled to anything I wanted—and I'm not talking about chips or ice cream.

Right after I was released from the hospital, I started fooling around with a twenty-something Canadian cameraman. It was a lot of fun, but he wasn't enough to satisfy me for long. This was the chance for me to go a little bit crazy, no? When you spend most of your teenage years in a nonremovable fat suit and then all of a sudden somebody unzips it, setting you free, you can't help but run around naked. It feels good to streak the world for a little while. And streak the world I did.

Why are kids always so embarrassed about bathtub pictures? I'm not ashamed to admit I think I look very cute in this one.

Here I am with my sister, Jennifer, riding a carousel. I was probably about three years old, and Jen was two. We had an amazing collection of Florence Eiseman applique dresses.

Just your average family portrait, taken in a Westchester parking lot. I'm on the left with the pigtails in the arms of my beloved Grandma Sylvia. My mom, Jill, is holding my sister, Jennifer, on the right. We were a very color-coordinated, patriotic bunch.

Here I am with my sister, Jennifer, around preschool age. I still can't believe I was so blond.

Here's the Lake family taking in some cabaret and frozen drinks (virgin, of course) after a long day visiting the set of *Cry-Baby* in Baltimore. My mom, Jill, is on the left, then me, my dad, Barry, and sister, Jen.

With John Waters, my Hollywood dad, on the set of *Hairspray*.

With the divine Divine, my Hollywood mom, on the set of *Hairspray*.

With Divine and Jerry Stiller, who played my parents in *Hairspray*, on the streets of Baltimore. See how big that hair was? Every strand was mine.

One of my favorite Polaroids of Divine and me.

On the set of *Working Girl* in 1988, the film I did right after *Hairspray*. My part was tiny but I was thrilled to be in a movie with Harrison Ford, Melanie Griffith, and Joan Cusack.

With Craig Sheffer, my love interest in *Babycakes,* on a New York City subway platform.

With Traci Lords and Johnny Depp on the set of *Cry-Baby*.

On the set of *Cry-Baby* with one my favorite guys from the crew a Susan Tyrrell, who played my au

Singing karaoke at my twenty-first birthda party. That's Cynthia Gibb in the black hat

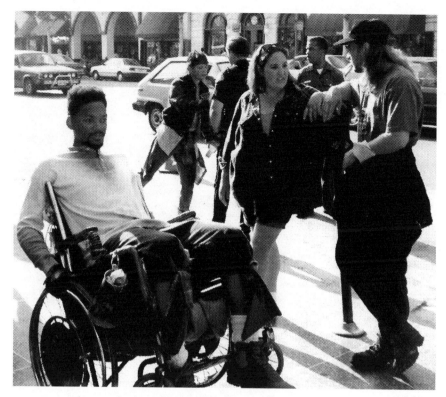

The set of *Where the Day Takes You* on Hollywood Boulevard, in 1991.
That's Will Smith in the wheelchair—it was his first feature film.

With my darling landlady Anne Klein in her backyard during my
ing-in-the-poolhouse period. I remember my rent there was $550 per month.

With Rob, during our happy newlywed days.

Shooting the promo for the upcoming launch of *The Ricki Lake Show* in Chicago, 1993.

In jail after being arrested for protesting the use of fur.
On my release I went straight to *The David Letterman Show*.
This is the warden holding the keys to all of the cells.

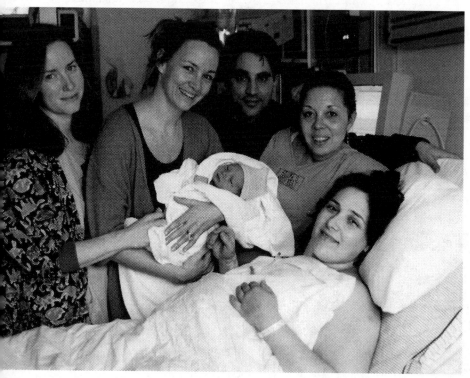

In the hospital with my incredible team just after the birth of my first baby, Milo.
With me are my nurse, my midwife, my doula, and Rob.

A reunion with Michael St. Gerard, my costar in *Hairspray*, and my landlady, Anne Klein, on a special episode of *The Ricki Lake Show*.

At the finish line of the Avon Breast Cancer 3-Day Walk.

Holding hands with my big boy, Milo,
[whi]le pregnant with Owen, my little one.
I gave birth just a few weeks later.

One of my favorite photos
of my boys and me.

Happy with Baby Owen at
his first birthday party.
Who could resist that face?

With the two other Tracy Turnblads: Nikki Blonsky, who played the role in the film adaptati of the Broadway musical, and Marissa Jaret Winokur, who originated the Broadway role. I lo skinny in that dress—earlier that morning was my photo shoot for the cover of *Us* magazir

With my boys, Owen and Milo, on the beach.

This was the photo shoot for the cover of *Us* magazine. I felt great that day.

And thank you to Norma Kamali for designing the world's most adorable red bathing suit.

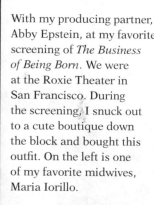

With my producing partner, Abby Epstein, at my favorite screening of *The Business of Being Born*. We were at the Roxie Theater in San Francisco. During the screening, I snuck out to a cute boutique down the block and bought this outfit. On the left is one of my favorite midwives, Maria Iorillo.

Rehearsal for *Dancing with the Stars*.

Christian in a moment of gratitude.
He always stops to smell the roses,
and the pine trees.

Christian and I on
our first trip to Ibiza.

Christian and I atop a hill in Ibiza,
overlooking our favorite place in
the world.

Christian took this photo of me
the moment after we got engaged.

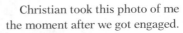

With Zena, the incredible makeup artist on *Dancing with the Stars*.

Don't worry, I didn't steal J.R.'s mirror ball trophy. This is a replica.

Backstage during week two. I danced the jive.

Backstage at *Dancing with the Stars* with fellow contestant Hope Solo and the amazing wardrobe team.

Paris, Christmas 2011, with Christian.

My boys and I a[t]
the Eiffel Tower in 20[

Christian and Owen accompanyin[g]
Marie and her little friend to the
CNN Heroes ceremony.

28

I'm a celebrity! I'll never really date online.

My Profile

I want: A hiking, artistic peacemaker to spend some major quality time with.

Lemme start out by saying that I love my life. A few words to describe me: Outgoing, vivacious, passionate, brave, hardworking, intelligent, spontaneous, positive, love to laugh, even if it's at my own expense, and 100 percent authentic.

At this point in my life, I know who I am and what I am looking for in a relationship.

I want a man who is:

Confident without being arrogant

Self-sufficient

Funny

Intelligent

Free spirited

Believes the glass is half-full

Romantic

Sexual

Adventurous

Physically fit

And attractive

Fairly straightforward, right?

Wait until you see what the universe came up with.

29

*I'll never get dissed by an
unemployed street musician.*

I've always had a soft spot for musicians, so when I got an e-mail from a cute guy named Jake who called himself a "singer-songwriter," I agreed to go out with him. Before we met in person, he sent me files of his music, and I honestly thought he was really good. He sounded like Dave Matthews. I imagined the two of us writing music together, debating the merits of our favorite Beatles songs, reaching climax in two-part harmony.

Corresponding online was effortless. At some point before our meeting, though, I knew I'd have to tell him who I was. So he wouldn't feel ambushed when we got together in real life, I wrote, "Look, I'm kind of a famous person." I was surprised by how embarrassed I felt to say this in writing. Part of me didn't want to assume Jake knew who I was, while another part of me thought, *He damn well better know who I am!* Even so, I was re-luctant to reveal my identity, because I thought it would change our dynamic one way or another. Either he'd be intimidated, or he'd think I was being arrogant and pretentious using my name to try to impress people.

But Jake took my confession in stride, saying he'd thought I might be a public person, but that he wasn't sure and it didn't affect his feelings for me one way or the other. Perfect answer, right?

We made plans to have our first date at a karaoke bar. This was great for me because I can kick ass at karaoke. Ask any-body. Even better, I knew Jake could sing too. What's sexier than a little friendly competition? A hot duet, right? That's what I was thinking!

Although Jake wasn't quite as good looking in real life as he was in his photographs—*they never are, ladies, they never are*—we shared an undeniable chemistry. Add to that the fact that he was a bona fide amazing singer. I was undeniably interested.

He seemed like the perfect dude with whom to get my virtual feet wet: wide-eyed, young, singing on Santa Monica's pedestrian-friendly Third Street Promenade, in the service of his art. Selling CDs in order to buy groceries. How romantic, right? I surprised even myself as I thought, *Wow, I'm kinda lik-ing this guy!*

There was one tiny blip: while on his profile he'd seemed trim and fit, Jake in person was a little bit chubby. Rather than turn me off, this inconsistency endeared him to me, because it made me feel super-hot, like I had the upper hand in the re-lationship, since I was in better shape (at least temporarily). I knew I wouldn't have to worry about disappointing Jake in any way. Even though this may sound ridiculous, any fat or formerly fat girl can relate to what I'm about to say: a fit and handsome guy—no matter how stupid, unsuccessful, or morally vacant he might be—can make even the most accomplished woman feel like shit about her body and, subsequently, herself in general, if he wants to.

As our first date was coming to a close, I heard a voice deep inside me saying, *Don't ruin the potential with this guy by taking things too far tonight.* That voice told me that I must really like him.

You're not going to have sex with him, Ricki, I told myself. *You're not going to do anything. You're not even going to kiss him! You're going to say good night and get in your car. Practice having a normal first date. You can do it. Don't be a slut.*

As our evening came to a close, Jake hugged me, and told me that he liked me a lot and that he would love to take me out again.

Score! Being demure really does work!

In e-mail over the next couple of days, Jake gushed on and on about all the places he wanted to take me—*This restaurant is amazing because it's close to this jazz club where we can go and listen to music afterward, blah blah*—and I was swooning a little bit. Over the next couple of days, I found myself thinking about Jake, wondering what he was up to, what he was into. I considered my feelings for him over and over again. *I like the way he asked me for the second date while we were still on the first. I like that he's a gentleman. I like that he's a starving—okay, if not starving, then struggling—artist.*

I let myself imagine Jake and me as a couple—an unlikely pair, to be sure, but unconcerned about other people's judgmental opinions. This was going to be fun!

My second date with Jake took place just a couple of nights after the first. We went to have dinner at his favorite Italian place, and then we walked over, hand-in-hand, to a little bar in Santa Monica to listen to some live blues.

Sitting in the back of this dark club, grooving to what was inarguably some pretty shitty music, Jake and I made out like teenagers. And feeling a wee bit brazen, which is not out of character for me, truth be told, I whispered in Jake's ear, "This music sucks. I want to hear *your* music."

So he whispered back, "Do you want to go to your place?" And then, when I was silent, he hesitated for a moment and suggested, "My place?"

And I said, "Yeah! Let's go to your place!"

His place was the obvious choice for a number of reasons. First, it was within walking distance. Second, even though I liked the guy, I wasn't quite ready for him to know where I lived.

So we walked over to his place. Two words suffice to describe it: a bed.

That's all poor Jake had room for: a bed! We walked in, and there was a bed, and a guitar, and a bathroom. That was it. Immediately I thought, *Oh, my God, I can never show this guy where I live!*

You know how some people say they live in "a garden apartment"? This guy lived in a "closet apartment."

I sat down on—what else?—the bed, and Jake put on some music. We fooled around a little bit, and then he started taking his clothes off.

Now in case I haven't yet made this clear, I prefer to have romantic relations with hot guys. Not okay-looking guys, not weird-looking guys, but hot guys, plain and simple. Maybe I'm overcompensating for having been the girl who couldn't get the hot guys for all those years, but I don't really care. Now I can get them, so I do.

As nice, talented Jake with the miniature apartment was taking off his clothes, I was like, *His flesh is so soft! His skin isn't exactly what you'd call tight. In fact, it's a little bit . . . loose. And yet—I still really like him! Go, me! I'm not as judgmental as I thought!*

I cannot believe I am actually turned on by this out-of-shape guy. This represents major progress. I am growing secure enough in myself not to need to bask in the hotness of my sexual partners. I am finally able to like a man for who he is, not what he looks like. Oh, my God. I'm actually kind of into him!

I stayed in Jake's closet bedpartment until about one in the morning. We had sex twice. I was really liking him, and before I left, we talked about getting together again. He had a busy weekend, but suggested we go out the following Monday night. So we made a plan, and I was looking forward to it. I left my favorite hat at his place by mistake, but I knew I'd see him in a couple of days, so I didn't worry about it.

Cut to what I saw on Monday. Let me give you a hint: it wasn't Jake. It was, *Dear* Jake. A Dear John letter. From Jake. Lord of the Closet Bedpartment had dumped me before we could even go on our third date.

I'd reprint the letter here entirely, but I don't want to violate Jake's privacy, and besides, it's more fun if I get to retell it myself.

Basically, Jake told me that he had really been struggling in trying to decide which mode of communication would be best suited to contacting me—e-mail, phone, in-person hang-out, text, carrier pigeon—and had decided that sending me an e-mail was the only way to ensure that his words wouldn't get misconstrued. (Yes, the preamble to his note was at least that wordy, maybe twice as wordy. It also included his thoughts on why honesty is indeed the best policy, which I will spare you here.) He told me that he thought he was ready to start dating again, he really did, but unfortunately what had happened to him the last time he thought he was ready to date was happening again: he was consumed by memories of his ex-girlfriend. Mind you, this was not an ex-girlfriend he mentioned to me on either of our dates. He didn't even mention ever having had a girlfriend. Given the size of his apartment, it was hard for me to imagine that Jake had ever been alone with another human being.

Jake went on to say that he didn't usually let things move so fast, physically speaking, but that he and I enjoyed an un-deniable chemistry. He didn't regret having slept with me, he wrote (thanks?), but he had to admit an honest concern. He wor-ried that if his ex-girlfriend were to call while we were in the heat of passion, asking to discuss their former relationship, he would take the call. This, he decided, simply was not fair to me. (I agree, of course—I prefer not to be tossed aside during a pas-sionate moment in favor of a theoretical phone call from my partner's ex.)

"I don't have any desire to introduce drama into your life, which is going great, from all I gather," he wrote. "I'm sorry that I unintentionally misrepresented the state of my heart the other night. You never get anywhere without trying, and I thought— I mean, I was ready to give it a try! I mean, fuck! It's been over

eight months now. When does something like that change?"
I don't know, Jake. Maybe when you stop treating post-second-
date breakups as though they were divorces?

He coughed out a couple more paragraphs of apologies,
then a plea that we might one day be friends. "Once again," he
said, "I'm sorry for the drama that I have already caused." Poor
guy. To him, this was drama? It's OK, Jake. I forgive you.

He ended by saying that he'd get me back my hat in whichever way would make me feel most comfortable. And then, "Regardless of what happens from here, I'm not going to discuss
what happened between us to anyone. I respect your right to
personal privacy."

May I remind you that I've spent a grand total of two eve-
nings with this guy, but I have now done dramatic readings of
his e-mail a minimum of 500 times. He saved me from the pain
of feeling rejected by acting sappy and inappropriately attached.

*Dear Jake, You're not gonna tell anybody, but I'm gonna tell
everybody!*

I could barely stop laughing long enough to write him:
"Hey! No worries! Good luck to you! Please send my hat to my
mailing address, thanks!"

He wrote back immediately, "You got it."

Not like he was waiting to hear from me or anything.

I never expected to hear from him again, but around
Christmastime, he wrote me an apology, going on and on about
how sorry he was.

I was like, *Please, dude! You gave me the best comedy routine, and all I had to do was sleep with you?*

Seriously, though, he was a very sweet and talented guy,
and I hope he's been able to make it work with his ex.

30

I'll never fall for some lunatic's scam.

Far from turning me off to online dating, my bizarre experience with Jake felt like spring training. Now I was fired up and ready for the big leagues. On to the next guy!

Things started out unremarkably with Brian, but for the fact that he seemed too good to be available and dating online. His profile and photos reminded me of someone Carrie Bradshaw might have gone out with on *Sex and the City*. He was a handsome British playwright with dark curls, olive skin, and a pair of ice-blue eyes that radiated an almost otherworldly twinkle.

Our initial correspondence was a dream. Brian said all the right things, seemed to be interested in me for just the right reasons—or at least not specifically for the wrong ones, anyway—and he managed, at the same time, to make me feel smart and also like he had a lot to teach me.

After we had sent a few e-mails back and forth, I dropped the F-bomb. Dropping the F-bomb, in my case, is telling someone I'm famous.

"Look, I'm somebody you might know," I typed reluctantly, cringing. When it comes to anonymous online dating, the fame thing is so awkward. You don't want somebody to *like* you for it; you don't want somebody *not* to like you for it. I directed him to YouTube to watch a clip about my documentary. That's how I revealed who I was.

Brian's reply couldn't have been better had I scripted it myself:

"I'm English, Ricki," he wrote. "Fame alone doesn't impress me. Making a great political documentary, however . . ."

Since I had spent the last few years of my life working on *The Business of Being Born,* I was thrilled that Brian saw it as a major accomplishment. I needed anyone who stepped into my world romantically to understand that being an advocate and documentary filmmaker were at the core of my identity, more than anything else I had done in my career.

Brian said that he understood what it meant to be passionate about social issues; he had his own obsessions. Brian really seemed to appreciate the fact that I had chosen to take a detour away from the mainstream media and turn toward pursuing something that mattered to me on a core level. He himself had chosen to write plays to be produced in festivals such as the Edinburgh Festival Fringe rather than making bank in the mainstream drama-writing scene, because the most important thing in the world to him was integrity.

This man was genuinely into me, and I was definitely intrigued by him. Had the universe finally sent me somebody up to the challenge of being my equal partner? Was I finally ready to admit that a partner—and not just a fuck buddy—was what my heart was really looking for?

Once we met, the chemistry between me and Brian was electric. We went from having our first date to being boyfriend and girlfriend within a week. Soon we were spending all our time together talking about social justice, Shakespeare, and romantic ideals. You know those scenes in period piece movies, where the young soldier is courting the debutante and they spend all their time lying around on picnic blankets under shady trees, feeding each other fruit? We were like that.

As I got to know Brian he told me about some of the issues that were important to him. He had a deep distrust of all Western governments, believing that those in power purposefully withheld the truth from the people they governed. He had spent a good deal of time researching what he referred to as "the 9/11 conspiracy" and managed to be pretty convincing in his assertion that none of us really knows the whole story about what happened on that awful day and ever since.

I was a little bit suspicious when Brian shared this view with me—visions of Mel Gibson stalking Julia Roberts in *Conspiracy Theory* flashed through my head—but as a personal challenge, I tried not to judge him. We're all so jaded these days, especially in Hollywood, that we often dismiss those with strong, offbeat opinions as "psycho" or "clueless." Maybe this guy was just honest and English and *right*. I mean, he was so sexy.

By the time we were just a couple of weeks into our relationship, Brian had decided that I was his muse. He claimed to find me so beautiful—body and soul—that he was moved to "create art" whenever I was around. He wrote poetry and songs about me and took photographs of me lounging around my house half-naked in a cowboy hat.

Brian asked me if I would star in a video he wanted to make to accompany a song he'd written. The subject matter was intense—a tragic story that revolved around a man losing the love of his life—but he couldn't imagine anybody else in the role but me. He played me the song on his acoustic guitar, singing gently in his smooth baritone, "Open your eyes, everything's here for you. The most beautiful sight, all of your dreams came true." I'm a sucker for musical talent, and knowing Brian had written this heartfelt song in my honor made me swoon. *Of course I'd do his video.*

The storyline for the video was sort of complicated. A beautiful married couple is so in love that it seems that no harm can come to them. They frolic around a bucolic estate, laughing, holding hands. We are privy to their most intimate moments and gestures: she bites her lip, they walk hand in hand in slow motion, her engagement ring glints magically in the sunlight. One day they take a walk in the quaint little town where they live. The woman notices a sign advertising free swine flu vaccinations. She wants them to partake. What could be more important than their health, with a long future ahead of them? He doesn't want the vaccine, and he doesn't want her to get it either. She insists. She wants to be invulnerable to the epidemic so they can be together forever. He begs her not to be vaccinated. She feels the responsibility to stay healthy for him. She enters the clinic alone. He's wracked with anguish. She gets the vaccination. He recoils in horror. Next time we see her is in the hospital. Next time we see him, she's dead.

Pretty intense, right? And more than a little bit weird. Writing a song about your loved one's succumbing to the supposed conspiracy of H1N1 in a desperate effort to save the world? Unusual, to say the least. But I certainly had no exhaustive knowledge of the topic. Maybe Brian was right? So many people had dismissed my beliefs in childbirth choices without doing any hard thinking, and I didn't want to be as ignorant as they were.

Making a little movie with Brian was beyond romantic, and I gave it my all. I knew that the glow I got from our relationship would be visible onscreen, and I couldn't wait to see it.

My friends thought the whole thing was a little strange. They warned me that Brian might be too offbeat to trust so wholeheartedly, that something was *off.* I didn't listen, telling myself that they were just jealous that my amazing new boyfriend got to spend all this time with me that I used to spend with them and that we were making important art together.

After about a month spending all our time together, I noticed that Brian had started getting moody. He had posted our video on YouTube, but nobody seemed to really understand it. I had plans to go to England with Milo to do some birth stuff, and I invited Brian to come, thinking it would cheer him up to be back home.

I bought him a first-class ticket, along with mine and Milo's. When we got to the airplane, we discovered that our pod seats—the kind that recline and have a built-in entertainment system—were in different rows. Being inseparable, we begged our neighbors to switch seats with us so we could sit together.

After a comedic game of musical chairs, Brian and I were happily ensconced next to each other for the long flight. Just before take-off, he turned on his TV. Let the transcontinental veg-out begin!

Except his TV didn't work. And the flight attendant couldn't fix it.

"Switch seats with me," Brian told—or rather, commanded—me.

"Are you kidding?" I asked.

"No," he replied, stone-faced.

"No way!" I responded. "Why should I be the one with the broken TV?" (*Isn't it enough that I'm the one paying for all this?*)

"Because you're going to take an Ambien and pass out for the whole flight, and then I'll be awake and alone."

"Not true. Not switching. Go fuck yourself!" Okay, so I didn't really say that last bit, but I was thinking it.

Contrary to what you might think, Brian did not sit next to me sulking for the entire flight. He was perfectly content, watching movies. Because he insisted that his original seat-changing partner—the gentleman who had been gracious enough to relocate so that we could sit together, as well as the person next to him—change back! Brian simply refused to be stuck with the broken TV.

The whole thing was mortifying. I wanted to die. So I took an Ambien, watched some opening credits, and promptly fell asleep.

Once we got to England, I met Brian's mother. For a moment, I felt as though I could see him through her eyes: this man was strange and hard to manage, and she was relieved someone had finally arrived to take him off her hands. I panicked a little but pushed through the feeling.

One day when I couldn't find Brian at the hotel where we were staying, I wandered down to the gym and found him making a mysterious call from a hidden phone. I asked who he was talking to, and he just answered vaguely, "Work." For the first time, I started to doubt my instincts that he was the one for me. But I soldiered on as his companion.

Soon after we got back to LA, it was my forty-first birthday. I love birthdays and I love having parties, and it was really nice to have such a handsome and intelligent date at my side. Brian wrote me a special song and sang it to me in front of everybody. It was called "Let's Just Get Married." I could tell my friends were suspicious of him, but I didn't let this keep me from having a great time, and feeling loved—in the moment, anyway. *Maybe we should just get married? He's so good-looking!*

The next day, basking in a postparty glow, I fantasized about my life with Brian. I could get over all the weird stuff—he was so smart, and so handsome, and so into me. Maybe I would develop one of those ridiculous but amazing British accents people get when they marry British people! Maybe we would take a yearly vacation to the Cotswolds! Maybe H1N1 really was a government conspiracy!

In the midst of this reverie, I got a phone call from a friend. "Ricki, go on Facebook."

"Huh?"

"Go on Facebook. I need to show you something."

In order to see what she wanted me to see, I needed to log in under her user name, which was a pain. "Just tell me what you want to tell me," I begged her. "This is taking forever."

I persevered, though, and soon it was clear why: one of my friend's Facebook friends had posted a series of blissfully romantic photos, starring her . . . and Brian.

"Are you effing KIDDING me?" I screamed.

"I'm just the messenger!"

Poor friend.

This was the last straw. Even though I was still the tiniest bit under Brian's spell, I knew I needed to end things. How had I let this happen? It was simple—I had wanted a boyfriend for my forty-first birthday. I had my blinders on, and I let Brian take advantage of me. I was doing such a poor job of looking out for myself that my friend Josh swears I drove him into a depression. I was the crazy one brainwashed by this terrible guy, and Josh was the one who went on medication.

Once I was finally able to look in the mirror and realize that I had been brainwashed, I made plans to meet Brian for dinner that evening so I could end things. "This isn't working," I said, with remarkable composure. "This is over."

His lip quivered, and I remembered one of the lines from his song: "If you leave me, I'll die." I crossed my fingers he hadn't meant it. This guy was seriously unstable.

After dinner, Brian didn't even bother walking me to my car. If I hadn't been sure of my decision to let go of him initially, I sure was at that moment.

"No hard feelings," I told him. "I learned a lot about myself."

The next day, I got a text from him. "It's been a great experience," he said. "I'd love to see you one more time to give you back your stuff and a hug."

I texted back, "No hard feelings," and picked a place for us to meet. A little Italian spot on San Vicente in Brentwood, with an amazing $18 lunch special.

"Oh, it's very expensive," he replied.

"My advice is, don't order the steak," I texted back.

"Touché," he said.

I met him the next day. Throughout lunch, I couldn't take my eyes off the massive blemish that had appeared smack dab in the middle of his forehead. Earlier in our relationship, he might have been able to convince me that it was a third eye. Yuck. I finally saw him for who he was.

He left our lunch, sobbing, on Saturday at 2:00 PM.

The next day I got a phone call from my friend Erin. "Go on Facebook as me!" she said. "Here's my login."

I went to her page and discovered at the top of her news feed a photo of a girl I did not recognize, cheek to cheek with Brian at sunset. I was flabbergasted, not only because it was now ultraclear he had been two-timing me, but also because, in the photo, his face was marred by the very same zit by which I'd been so horrified during our lunch. That meant he'd left our lunch sobbing and begging me to take him back—what an actor!—then drove straight to Venice in time to enjoy a romantic sunset with this other girl.

That was the moment I said to myself, "This dude's going down."

I wanted to warn Girlfriend #2 about his two-timing ways, so I sent her a message on Facebook. It wasn't really a surprise that she wanted nothing to do with me—she thought she was in love! Two weeks later, she called me and said their relationship had fallen into pieces just as ours had.

I decided to have a bit of fun with Brian—put the cherry on top of our ridiculous relationship, so to speak. I knew a private investigator from my divorcing days, so I paid him to sneak into Brian's building and stick a note under his door that read: "Ms. Lake wants the footage back." Brian, terrified, agreed to meet up with him, and they went through Brian's computer trashing video files. Hell if I was going to let that bird flu video end up on TMZ.

I got to grace him with one last phone call, during which I said, "I'll make sure you never do this to another woman again."

"What does that MEAN?" he pleaded for me to answer, desperately. I think he assumed that I was calling the Immigration and Naturalization Service to get him deported, and I saw no reason to correct his assumption. What I did was call match.com customer service and get him banned for life. I'm willing to bet a green card I'll never see those crazy eyes—or that third-eye zit—again.

31

I'll never date anybody famous.

At this point, as I'm sure you can imagine, I decided I was through with Internet dating. No judgment to those for whom it works. For me, the risks simply outweighed the benefits. I decided to take my manhunt back into the real world.

But first I had a lot of work to catch up on.

The Business of Being Born was doing even better than everyone had expected, and I decided to do another round of TV appearances to make sure the wave continued. (It bears mentioning that when I say the movie was doing well, I mean that people were seeing and responding to it. We haven't yet come close to breaking even financially—who knows if we ever will?) For the first time ever, I wasn't at all insecure about how I would look on camera while doing the talk show circuit, because I was the thinnest I'd ever been. I appeared on the cover of *Us Weekly* in a red bathing suit (one-piece—I wasn't *that* skinny). And I heard three beautiful words at least once daily: "You're too skinny."

What's the opposite of a backhanded compliment? A front-handed insult? Whatever you want to call it, "you're too skinny" is music to my ears. It's the phrase that gives me more confidence than any other. When I'm "too skinny," I get treated like a different person. Men look at me in a different way. There's such a difference between going from heavy to average sized, versus from average sized to "thin-thin." People congratulate you on the former, but the latter makes them jealous. And I have to admit, I don't really mind being envied.

So I was in New York at the height of my hotness, and I was ready to have some fun. The night before I was set to appear on *The View* to talk about the documentary, a friend invited me to a publicist's party at some cool downtown club. I had no plans and I was single, so I figured I'd go for one drink, then rest up in preparation for the show.

When I arrived at the party early and alone, I was ushered into the VIP area, where I sat down, ordered a cocktail, and waited for my friend to show up. Right after I settled in, a very tall, handsome, well-known musician arrived, alone too. I recognized this guy, as I had long respected both his songwriting and his technical abilities.

He smiled at me, and I smiled back. Soon he had come over to my table.

"I've always had a crush on you," he said, grinning but not kidding. His admission thrilled me more than just a little bit. I was almost a decade older than this guy, and he had a reputation for dating extraordinarily beautiful women. His acknowledging his attraction to me was better than being on the cover of *Us*, it was like being on the cover of *Vogue*.

"Well, the feeling is mutual!" I replied with a giggle, and

before I knew it, this guy, whom I'll call Mr. Charisma, was kind
of making the moves on me. I was sitting in that club, trying to
suppress my shit-eating grin and thinking, *I cannot believe this
is my life. Are you kidding me, universe?*

Mr. Charisma and I talked, talked, and talked—nonstop.
There was so much to talk about. He had this whole bar set up
on the table, the kind of bottle service extravaganza nightclubs
love to lavish on celebrities and big spenders, and he kept making me cocktails.

Soon I was drunk enough to make fun of some of his more
well-known ex-girlfriends. "How could you spend such a long
time with such a ditz?" I asked brazenly. Mr. Charisma was
a good sport; he said she was really nice and not as dumb as
people think.

Then somehow the conversation turned to the topic of theoretical sex. Between the two of us.

"I can tell you're really sexual," he whispered to me, grinning. I just smiled demurely in tacit agreement.

The two of us were enjoying a crazy chemistry, and there's
no question that at that moment, if the opportunity had come
up, we would have gotten down.

But it was getting late, and since I had an early call time for
The View, I told Mr. Charisma I had to leave.

"Come meet me at Gold Bar downtown," he whispered, as
he entered his cell number into my phone.

"Okay," I replied, flattered and not wanting to disappoint
him (even though I knew that the chances of my actually showing up were slim to none). I jumped in a cab that was heading
toward my hotel, along with the friend who'd invited me to the
party and another friend of hers, a writer.

As soon as our cab pulled away from the curb, Mr. Charisma started texting me.

"Come meet me! Come meet me!" he wrote, and were it any other night, I would have. But it was important to me to be fresh and rested for *The View*. I take Barbara Walters seriously.

"I don't think I can come tonight," I replied. "I have to work early in the morning. How about tomorrow night or the one after?"

"Yes!" he wrote back instantly. "We need to go out!"

At this point, I was dying of excitement, and I decided to tell the two girls in the cab with me what was going on. "Mr. Charisma is texting me!" I squealed with delight, "What should I write?" Both were duly impressed and happy to give counsel. Soon I was texting him back by committee. It felt as if we were having a tenth-grade slumber party in the back of a taxicab.

In no way did I feel out of line bringing my friend and her friend into the loop. Everyone had seen Mr. Charisma and me sitting together at the party, and it was obvious that he was making the moves on me.

That night, I went back to the hotel and got to sleep early, as planned. The next morning, it was off to *The View*. I was a guest cohost, so I got to interview the other guests rather than be interviewed myself.

It turned out that one of the guests I was interviewing was a former teen movie idol with whom I'd been a little bit in love—just like every other girl on the planet—for most of my life. I could tell, even on air, that there was more than just a friendly vibe between us.

After the show, sure enough, he made the moves on me. I blew off Mr. Charisma to hang out with—let's call him "Sensitive Teen Heartthrob."

So Sensitive Teen Heartthrob and I stayed up all night talking, having a really great time. The whole thing was almost like an out-of-body experience; I kept looking at Sensitive Teen Heartthrob's face and imagining myself in one of his movies.

Now this guy, who happens to be exceptionally intelligent and a lot of fun, went against pretty much everything I'm into. I tend to stay away from famous people. But I loved the characters I had seen this guy play so much that it almost felt as if I knew him. My life was becoming *so ridiculously cool.*

The next morning, I was scheduled to do *The Howard Stern Show.* It was my first time, and I was excited. The first thing Howard said when I arrived at the studio was, "So what's the deal with you and Mr. Charisma?"

My mind still on Sensitive Teen Heartthrob, I was like, "What the hell are you talking about?"

And Howard replied, "What, you're not a New Yorker anymore? Don't you read Page Six? Don't you read the *Post*?"

Apparently the third girl in the cab—the one I didn't know, the writer—worked as a gossip reporter for the city's most widely read daily newspaper. She had printed that Mr. Charisma and I had been all over each other at a party and that even after we'd left separately, we kept texting each other nonstop. It was weird to have my privacy violated like that, but I played it cool. "Oh yeah, Howard—Mr. Charisma is a really nice guy. I met him the other night, and he's really cool."

"Text him right now! Text him right now!" Howard said like an over-eager high school gossip queen.

I was apprehensive, because I barely knew the guy. And I'd never even had a flirtation with somebody who was famous—not until Sensitive Teen Heartthrob, anyway. As for Mr. Charisma, we didn't even kiss. It felt odd to be talking about something that hadn't happened.

If you've ever listened to Howard, you know that he's pretty ADD, so soon, thankfully, he had changed the subject to my recent weight loss. (What else?) "Oh, my God, Ricki, you're so hot," Howard said. "I would bend you over right here!" Inappropriate but flattering. Howard has this amazing ability to say the crudest things and remain totally lovable.

He's also obsessed with weight, like many other Jewish guys, who must pick up the fixation from their mothers. "What do you weigh? What do you weigh?" he asked me with frantic fascination.

"Um, I think I weigh, like, 126 pounds?" I replied. It was hard to believe, even though it was true.

"You're hot," Howard told me. "I'm gonna give you that. You're like, so smoking hot, *I'd* do you."

(Gee, thanks.)

"But if you lost 10 pounds, you would be that much hotter.'"

It was crazy. For the first time, I didn't feel insulted by a critical comment being made about my body. I didn't think he was a dick or anything, but his comment was patently ridiculous.

"Howard, I'm a size 4," I told him, in the tone of voice reserved for kindergarten teachers telling kids it's naptime. "I'm so small. I don't get smaller than this."

"I'm telling you: you're HOT!" Howard said. "I'm agreeing with you! You're damn smoking hot—"

I smiled with satisfaction.

"But if you lost 10 more pounds . . ."

I rolled my eyes in mock disapproval. What Howard said really didn't offend me. I thought it was funny. More important,

I think the role he plays on the radio is a fictional character. He's not really so hypercritical and objectifying. Obviously the kind of language he uses is perpetuating the message that we are not good enough unless we're stick thin and suffering from some eating disorder, and that's not okay. But his fans would revolt if he ever started to change.

As for what they say about how you can never be too rich or too thin, the rich and thin take this saying seriously. That is why they are so rich and so thin. The fact that I still had to put up with all the weight bullshit, even when I weighed a piddly 126 pounds, made me realize that all the time I'd been criticized for being fat, I should have tried not to take it personally.

I was proud of myself for surviving an appearance on *Howard Stern*, and with flying colors. What I didn't know, though, was that Mr. Charisma was a loyal listener, and by the next day, he was accusing me of being an opportunist, using his name for publicity. He implied that I had somehow made more out of our flirtation than it was just so I could talk about it in the press.

What Mr. Charisma said hurt me deeply because I am the opposite of an opportunist. I was mortified about what had appeared in the *Post,* but when I was giggling like a teenager in that cab, I had no idea I was being ambushed by a gossip columnist. And Mr. Charisma had put the moves on me in public, with all these witnesses around. Which one of us was the opportunist?

In order to put a stop to the whole thing and save myself any further embarrassment, I told anybody and everybody that nothing had happened between us. The whole thing was a cringefest, but I assumed Mr. Charisma would figure out that I'd been played by the press.

The following weekend, I was back in LA and attending a

movie premiere. I was happy to be home and had been looking forward to a fun night out on the town. As I made my way
across the red carpet, whom did I notice but Mr. Charisma? I
was happy to see him, eager to get any post-Howard awkwardness out of the way.

I went up to him to say hi, and he immediately started yell-
ing at me in front of everyone. The whole thing seemed to be
happening in slow motion.

"You're an opportunist," he said.

Was this really happening?

"You have such a big mouth!"

"RICKI! OVER HERE!" yelled the paparazzi.

I tried to smile for the cameras, but I was absolutely devastated. My cheeks were on fire with humiliation.

The next day, even though I didn't think I had done anything wrong, I was desperate to clear the air. I cannot stand
confrontation or having anger hang between me and—well,
pretty much anyone. I abhor being uncomfortable.

My friend Robin, who is amazingly articulate and calm in
the face of social trauma, helped me write Mr. Charisma a long
text that explained exactly what had happened from my point of
view. I told him that I wasn't really used to getting so much attention and that if I had committed any crime at all, it was just
being overenthusiastic about our flirtation while trapped in a
taxi with a girl who happened to make her living as a gossip columnist. I told him that I've maintained a lifelong rule of never
dating famous people, and that this situation illustrated why:
things can get so easily misconstrued.

To Mr. Charisma's credit, he wrote me back immediately
with a very understanding message—almost an apology: "What

an interesting predicament you find yourself in, being newly hot, and not knowing how to navigate the social terrain. If you ever see me again, please don't cringe."

What a relief to know I hadn't been totally wrong about this guy. It was a really nice ending. I don't ever have hard feelings; in fact, if I ever see him again, forget cringing—I'm going in for a hug! At a certain point, when I wrote what I wrote, I needed to say what I needed to say. I didn't really care what he wrote back or whether he did, and I didn't plan to contact him again. I was kind of vindicated, seeing how he behaved in public: he was such an asshole. I got off easy; truthfully, I would have slept with him! I might have had my heart broken, because Mr. Charisma is nothing if not charismatic. Sure, he made an asshole of himself, but for that couple of hours I spent with him, he was a blast.

How could I so easily forgive someone so inconsiderate? When I think about what my ex-husband Rob and I had to go through with our divorce—how hard it was—I just think life is too short to hold on to negative feelings. That said, my brief encounter with Mr. Charisma was not the kind of experience I cared ever to repeat. From that point on, I vowed never to date men who were famous or at all interested in becoming famous. And forevermore, I'll prefer to have my men on the down-low, not mentioned on Page Six, thank you very much *New York Post*.

That said, I wasn't quite done with Sensitive Teen Heart-throb just yet. Much to my delight, he asked me to hang out when I returned to LA. He invited me over to his house, which was located in the best part of Malibu. I spoke to him on my cell phone as I drove there. That's when I discovered he was a teensy bit—eccentric.

"Is anybody following you?"

"What do you mean?"

"Like, paparazzi?"

"Um, no. Nobody cares where I'm going!"

"You're sure no paparazzi are coming?"

"Trust me. Nobody cares."

Once I got to his house, we had a great time. I liked his brain. His house was filled with great books and interesting artwork, and he wasn't afraid to be passionately political.

Soon Sensitive Teen Heartthrob and I were making out. I was surprisingly unnervous, despite the fact that kissing him felt like being in one of his movies. My internal monologue was hilarious: "Holy shit. Sensitive Teen Heartthrob is trying to get in my pants. What should I do?" It was so fun having power over someone my younger self had worshiped.

Our little romance ended after just three dates, but in the coolest of ways. Knowing it wasn't going to go anywhere, we were able to walk away from the whole thing as friends.

People have asked me whether I regret not sleeping with Sensitive Teen Heartthrob. I could have lived out my teenage cinematic fantasies in full!

In all honesty, I don't regret not going all the way. Driving to his house that night in the rain, I spoke to my friend Rachael.

"Should I sleep with him?" I asked her, breathlessly.

"Focus on how you want to feel about yourself in the morning," she answered, with typical elegance. I hung up and honestly asked myself her question. My answer? "I want Sensitive Teen Heartthrob to desire me sexually, and I also don't want to feel like a slut." Like Goldilocks and her porridge, I wanted things just right. And I fooled around just enough to get what I wanted.

32

I'll never be stronger than my father.

❧

At the same time I was trying out a bunch of romances with a bevy of different men, one of the most important men in my life was threatening to leave me. My father, Barry Lake, became mysteriously sick all of a sudden, and my sister Jennifer and I were forced to take care of him together. I'll always remember that crisis as the time we were most connected, as sisters.

Our dad suffered from a constellation of mysterious neurological symptoms: he developed a strange gait, forgot recent events, and showed an almost deranged affection for animals. Doctors first thought he had dementia, then ALS, then mad cow disease, then a brain tumor. Everyone had a different opinion, but the one thing they all agreed on was that he was dying.

My sister and I were devastated. Our dad had been the glue holding our family together, however loosely, and we depended on his strength, sense of humor, and intelligence to define who we were as members of the Lake family. Now he had become a helpless, almost pathetic creature who required around-the-clock care. For months, with the help of my incredible friends Molly, Josh, Simon, and Jen, we traveled from specialist to nursing home, trying to make what seemed to be my father's last days as bearable as possible. Although Jennifer and I had grown even more distanced in adulthood—she working in finance in the United Kingdom, me with my show and my boys—my father's struggle reminded us that we were on the same team. We united in our fight to save our dad, and by the time we got to the bottom of what was wrong with him—he had a nonconvulsive seizure disorder that would not kill him if managed properly—we had forged a new relationship as adult sisters rather than little girls.

Unfortunately, as my sister and I grew closer and my dad expressed his gratitude for our getting to the bottom of his medical mystery, my mother went missing in mind, body, and heart. Instead of standing by her husband as he suffered, she chose to leave him and their marriage, moving to Texas in pursuit of her life as a "Christian." My mother's choosing to abandon my dad at the time when he needed her most was the last straw for me. We are no longer in contact.

It has taken me a lot of soul searching to understand how I can identify so strongly as a mother yet feel no connection to my own. I'm sorry to say I doubt she has done the same kind of self-exploration. I am not ashamed to say that part of me was hoping her new Texas home would get scooped up by a tornado during storm season.

33

*I'll never be happier than
I am in this beach house.*

All that time dating like a maniac ended up to be, thankfully, no more than a phase. As I spent some quiet time with myself, I realized that what I was looking for with all those weird guys was external validation. Each time some dude was attracted to me, it felt like a win. Attraction as competition. Even though I saw that teensy number on my bathroom scale, I wasn't sure whether I was thin enough to be pretty yet. I needed men to gauge my attractiveness for me.

All my life I've been most concerned with pleasing others. Being acceptable to others had long been the only thing that made me feel acceptable to myself.

But when I had finally had enough, I decided to take a break from dating altogether and figure out what I really wanted to do next in my life. My father's sudden illness had been a terrifying wake-up call. I wanted to spend some quality time with my sons and my friends. I needed to breathe a big sigh of relief that my dad, despite all those health scares, was going to be okay.

In order to get some time away from it all, at the end of the summer of 2010, I rented a little beach house on the Pacific Coast Highway in a not-too-fancy section of Malibu. This place was tiny. I don't mean celebrity-tiny—I mean tiny-tiny. I had always loved being near the ocean, and even though this place was no more than a few miles away from our home in Brentwood, it was worlds apart.

To reach the Malibu house, which looked like no more than a surfer's hovel protected by a salt-corroded wooden gate from the outside, I would drive down Sunset Boulevard, away from the tony, mansion-filled enclave of Brentwood where my boys and I have lived for almost a decade, and through the winding streets of Santa Monica and Pacific Palisades, to where LA's most famous street dead-ends at the Pacific Coast Highway.

As my car wound west down Sunset on the drive to Malibu, the Pacific Ocean rose with majesty up to the horizon line, calm and deep and infinite. The end of the aptly named Sunset Boulevard is where the sun sets on the whole world, and catching a glimpse of it as day turns to night makes a person feel small in the best possible way.

I traveled the world's most scenic highway alongside hundred-thousand-dollar sports cars zooming toward Malibu, brimming over with the intoxicating combinations of youth, money, and power Hollywood is famous for. But rusted surf-mobiles traveled along the highway too, unembarrassed to slow down the Lamborghinis and Porsches nipping at their bumpers along the fast track. I grooved to the midtempo reggae snaking out the manual windows of those Volkswagen vans, the blissed-out glow of tan surfer feet stealing my attention from whichever impatient money mobile lurked in my rearview mirror.

Each time I looked down at my own hands, tan and free of polish, I was happy to feel that I finally had more in common with those surf bums than the moguls tailgating them. After my move to the beach, my daily uniform had changed from the claustrophobia of form-fitting red-carpet dresses and stilettos into the freedom of supersoft, oversized sweatpants and sheer tank tops: cotton play clothes that allowed me to move through the world with ease. I was happy to let my Dior and Stella McCartney dresses languish on their hangers. These days I got dressed in worn-out pieces still warm from the dryer, unself-conscious as a little kid in preschool. I even danced around the house in a tutu. (I swear. You can ask my housekeeper and surrogate sister, Iris.) What's more ridiculous than a woman of a certain age spinning around in pirouettes? Not much, and I liked it that way.

Renting a ramshackle house on the beach, even though it was just a few miles from my regular home in Brentwood, was evidence that I was giving myself permission to truly relax and explore. Staying in Malibu meant beach walks and bonfires, marshmallows and sing-alongs. The two-bedroom house, which really felt more like a houseboat than a land structure, was so small that when everybody was home, my boys and I *had* no choice but to spend quality time together.

Splayed all over a big white sectional as though it were our family bed, sometimes reading books or playing iPad games in silence, sometimes getting lost in endless family sing-alongs, we developed a closeness I hadn't remembered feeling since the boys were much younger. The walls of our home were windows, and the Pacific Ocean was our swimming pool. The house in Malibu was the perfect metaphor for living a natural and open life. Shoes and alarm clocks soon became unnecessary, we were living in such perfect rhythm with our surroundings.

I loved this funky little house so much that I wanted to buy it. It didn't matter that the place wasn't a "movie-star-caliber" residence; it had a stripped-down quality that liberated and inspired me and my family. Friends congregated on our rickety deck, telling stories and listening to the ocean deep into the night. The boys discovered shells, jellyfish, and a renewed closeness in their relationship on the perfect beach at our feet. The place had a contagious magic about it. I was looking forward to celebrating my forty-second birthday there, thinking of the freedom and expansiveness of the shoreline as a metaphor for how I wanted to live the next phase of my life.

Not many people understood why I would decide to leave my wonderful house in Brentwood vacant (and totally paid for), choosing instead to shell out thousands each month for the privilege of living in a glorified beach shack. I didn't expect everybody to get it, but I was in search of a less complicated life, desperate to remind myself how little I really needed in order to be happy. I had an inkling that paring down my surroundings and expectations would result in a state of inner calm, and as it turned out, my instincts were right.

This was the happiest I'd been in a long, long time. Taking a hiatus from high-pressure TV work to write a book and advocate for childbirth choices, I finally felt good about the current state of things. So many times before, I'd looked back on moments I'd already lived, wishing I'd been wise enough to appreciate them. Now, I was feeling like the Buddha of Brentwood: able to live, even luxuriate, in every moment as I was experiencing it.

I had been in this wonderful space—and headspace—for just over four weeks when it burned to the ground.

34

*I'll never go back to that big
Brentwood life again.*

Looking back on it now, the fire almost feels too cinematic to have happened in real life. My little family was the happiest it had been in a long time—dare I say, ever. We were spending full days and nights together, playing music, breathing fresh air, getting tons of exercise without even thinking about it. I realized that we depended much less on the trappings of the material world than our luxurious life in Brentwood had made it seem. More than once, the boys and I contemplated giving up our big house entirely, since that little house reminded us how we didn't really need anything besides one another.

But things changed in an instant. I haven't been able to

talk about the fire until now, for legal reasons, but here's what happened, once and for all. A few days before the fire, I bought a cute little lamp to put atop our glass coffee table. The lamp ran on biofuel, creating a pretty flame that was environmentally friendly. Because the beach house had no heating system, it got chilly at night, and the little lamp would give me and the boys a way to warm our hands.

The day of the fire, we got up around 7. Following the instructions that came with the lamp, I lit it using the lighter that had come in the package. Upon making contact with the fuel, the lamp sparked immediately, setting one of the couch cushions on fire. I ran into the kitchen to look for a fire extinguisher, but there was none to be found. I threw water on the fire, but it wouldn't go out. It was spreading quickly. I knew we didn't have much time, so I switched immediately into Mama Bear mode. My little one was already with me. "OWEN, GO WAKE YOUR BROTHER!"I screamed. He ran off. "MILO, MILO!"

I didn't know how quickly the fire would move, but I wasn't taking any chances. I called 911, and the boys and I, and our dog, Jeffie, ran out onto the Pacific Coast Highway.

The house was gone before the fire department arrived. Its destruction seemed to take place both in slow motion and on fast-forward. Although we had lost everything in the house, the boys and I were so grateful to have each other—to be alive, uninjured. It was as though the experience of living in the house itself had prepared us for the experience of losing it.

Every cloud has a silver lining—even if it's a cloud of smoke. In the days before the fire, I had met the man of my dreams. I just didn't know it yet.

Christian came into my life when my friend Jen bounded into our Malibu house and exclaimed, "Ricki, I met this really great new guy."

So is he single? I thought, in silence, and true to form, Jen read my mind.

"He's not your type."

If anyone knows the ins and outs of my type, it's Jen. She's been my best friend for more than twenty years, and I tell her everything. I mean, EVERYTHING. When I felt everybody wanted a piece of me, Jen thought only to give, not to take. She'd been there for my meteoric rise after *Hairspray*, then witnessed my precipitous fall when I got let go from *China Beach*. She was one of the only ones who stuck around back in the early 1990s when I didn't have a penny. Now Jen understood where I was in my heart and mind. "Why isn't he my type?" I asked. Although I was loath to admit it, I wanted to fall in love.

Jen told me that this guy was covered in tattoos and that I'd once met his former girlfriend at a party at her beach house. The girlfriend was a thin brunette who worked as a realtor, and I assumed she was Christian's only type. Even if I had been attracted to him back then, I would have put him out of my mind. If you're into pinched-face shiksas, you're not into me. It bears noting that at this point, I had put on about twenty pounds since bottoming out at 125. While I wasn't fat by any means, I was hiding out a little bit. Old patterns are hard to change.

As for Christian, I basically forgot Jen had mentioned him. I was having so much fun getting to know the Malibu crew out on the beach, watching in amazement as my boys and dog turned amphibious. Thanks to its proximity to Brentwood, our social life in Malibu was effortless. We already knew many people who lived there. One day Jen included Christian in a get-together of our core group of friends, along with her daughter, Ivy, whom I've known since she was born, her boyfriend at the time, and Josh and Simon, a couple who are basically my surrogate brother and brother-in-law. We all liked Christian immediately, and he became a fixture at our beach house board games and barbeques. I really loved being part of the Malibu community. It was the only place I've ever been in LA that nobody put on any airs—or even any makeup. Sweatpants and baseball caps were our uniform, and honesty was our policy. We were our true selves. We held nothing back.

During the amazing couple of weeks we spent in Malibu, I laid myself bare, sharing awful dating stories, frustrations with my ex, professional dilemmas. I was completely relaxed, making no effort whatsoever to be appealing or false in any way. My Malibu crew watched me stumble through an awkward flirtation with a cute Republican neighbor we'll call Malibu Mitch. There wasn't much between us, but I was flattered that he had asked me out and excited to get taken on some real dates. One of the pitfalls of having a high-profile career is that nobody ever seems to treat you like a regular girl.

While I told everybody I was excited about my date with Malibu Mitch, the whole thing was kind of a buzzkill. He was so polite that he didn't even try to hold my hand. What tipped me off to our lack of a future was that I didn't really care one way or the other whether he tried anything physical. Three nights before the fire, our little crew had an impromptu party, and even though I was officially there with Malibu Mitch, I found myself noticing what a nice guy Christian was, realizing it made me happy to have him around. As the group went to the local chili cook-off, then out to dinner, then played Apples to Apples, I decided that Christian and I needed to become good friends. He was hilarious and kind and easy to be around, and he made me feel safe.

The media coverage after the fire was shocking. I couldn't believe how many news outlets covered the story, and it was pretty painful to see how quickly the coverage slant shifted from concern for me and my family to blaming the victims. During a time when I thought everyone would be relieved that my family and I had escaped such a dangerous situation, instead, they were speculating about cause and motive.

After all the posttraumatic madness abated a bit, Jen told me that Christian had driven by the house a couple of times looking for me, and that he'd called to ask her how I was doing. *How thoughtful of him,* I thought, and told her to invite him to my birthday party later in the week, which would now be held at the big house. I was happy to be turning forty-two, but the feeling was bittersweet, since I'd long been fantasizing about celebrating in Malibu, and now the structure that seemed to contain my newfound happiness had been destroyed.

I couldn't believe that the magical feeling I'd had in Malibu—the sense that somehow my life was both full of infinite possibility and utterly complete—would no longer be mine. I was devastated. I had loved that little house.

Now, back in my Brentwood home, which felt too big all of a sudden, I worried I'd have to start finding myself all over again. This birthday was the kind that makes you feel nervous about the unknown, not the kind that makes you excited about what's going to happen next. I was prepared, though, to push all worry out of my mind and celebrate.

I arrived at my own birthday party in a short and sexy little dress, ready to have a cocktail, let loose, and let go of what had happened. Because of some careful planning, I knew I'd have my choice of suitors that night. I'd invited Malibu Mitch, as well as a couple of other guys with whom I'd had flirtations in recent years. Maybe other friends I'd invited would also come with single men in tow. Who knew? I would have my pick of make-out partners, depending on my mood. I definitely planned to get lucky on my birthday, and I didn't care whether whatever happened behind closed doors meant anything to either me or whomever I ended up with. I needed to blow off some steam.

A wide variety of eligible and interested men showed up at the party, and I flirted with each of them. I was pretty sure that any one of them would be receptive to my wishes, but I was still a little bit restless. Maybe I needed a shot of tequila? *Let's try it. Nope.* I was having fun, but felt as though something were missing. I chalked my lack of enthusiasm up to the trauma du jour—after all, MY HOUSE HAD JUST BURNED DOWN. *Give yourself a break, Ricki.*

Late in the evening, when many of my friends had already gone home and I was quite relaxed, I noticed a man coming through my front door. From the kitchen where I was standing, I could see about forty feet to the house's entrance, but it was dark and I could only make out shapes and shadows. Still, I recognized the tall, masculine silhouette, the thick, shiny blond hair, the broad shoulders.

It was my friend Christian!

I couldn't believe how happy I was to see him.

He made a beeline for me and his huge frame swallowed me up in a hug. I felt a charge between us that I had never noticed before, an energy that invigorated every one of my synapses.

As Christian and I had a drink together, the volume on the rest of the party dialed down, and it was just the two of us. We were captured by something magic: our hands kept finding one another in the most amazing sort of magnetism, my laugh got low and husky the way it does when I'm truly relaxed, his eyes scrunched up at their corners, and he looked at me in a way I'd never been looked at before.

The party thinned out, but we barely noticed, so captivated each of us was by the other. I invited him back to my room. We walked, hand in hand, down the hallway that connected my bedroom to Milo and Owen's. Along the walls were hundreds of photographs of me and my kids, and even though I was caught up in the moment, I also noticed the photos in a way I didn't usually. There was Milo graduating from his New York preschool; there was Owen dressed in his Pee-wee Herman getup for Halloween; there I was, a baby myself, just after getting my talk show. I felt an immense sense of gratitude for the way my life was turning out, no matter what happened romantically. My boys and I were the Three Musketeers, and I felt so lucky to be going through life with them at my side. No matter what, the three of us would be okay.

I led Christian past my massive bathroom into a bedroom

so beautiful that even after almost a decade living in it, I still can't believe it is actually mine. Huge and totally private, it has two walls made up of windows looking out on our vast yard, a cozy fireplace, gorgeous velvet seating, and, most important, a big, fluffy bed.

"I love being here with you," Christian said, and we started making out. He tasted amazingly familiar to me, and I couldn't get enough of him. Things got heated quickly. Then I mustered up my most serious voice and said, "Look, if we're going to do it, you're going to have to be my boyfriend. I'm not doing this as a one-night stand. You're too important to me."

He nodded and made an expression that told me, "Of course, I want to be your boyfriend." I couldn't believe how lucky I was. This was the best birthday ever! And with that, we settled down into the best night of lovemaking I'd ever had in my entire life.

And that was it. Christian was my birthday present from the universe.

It turns out that Christian had had his eye on me for a while. He'd been lying low, waiting to strike until the time was right. Christian had fallen in love with me while I was living in sweatpants. My guard had been down. I wasn't trying to be anything but my most organic self. Christian tells me now that from the moment he met me, he noticed that I had this confidence and spirit about me—this carefree, positive energy. That's what he responded to. I'm ashamed to admit now that when I first met Christian, he wasn't even on my romantic radar. If he had been, it's possible things might never have worked out. I might have screwed it up.

My usual way of "working" a guy I think is cute is to turn it on, make a big effort, wear something overtly provocative. I used to treat dating like an audition—maybe even more like a conquest. And I always, or almost always, got what I wanted.

But in Christian's case, I was so preoccupied with other inappropriate people—yes, plural, I'm not ashamed to admit it!—that he wasn't even someone to whom I really gave a second look. Christian got to know me as the person I am when I scratch my ass in the morning. And if he liked *that* girl, well then, everything else was gravy.

I had grown used to having these short-lived experiences with men I essentially turned into characters in my own story. I basically cast my own romantic interests, then projected all sorts of qualities onto these leading men. This was a lot of fun, sure, but you can't really expect to have a long-lasting, authentic relationship with someone who doesn't really exist.

I was able to convince even myself of these charades because before Christian, my affinity for men never came from feelings deep inside.

Instead, my temporary romantic obsessions always stemmed from craving validation from attractive men. *You're hot! You think I'm hot too, don't you?* Of course I realize now that I wasn't only objectifying myself by thinking this way, but also that I was objectifying the men I dated. At that point in my own development, I didn't appreciate men as fully developed people whom I could truly connect with but as nourishment for my self-esteem.

Thinking about this now, it all sounds so shallow, but for

a long time, my system seemed to work for me: I had fun, and I was pretty sure I was happy. Until, that is, Christian made love to me on my forty-second birthday. You know how people with poor eyesight say they never knew how clear the world could look until the day they got their glasses? Being with Christian the first time was that level of life-changing. He said he saw me as a phoenix, rising from the ashes of the fire. I love that Christian always sees the strength in me. That he's captivated and invigorated, rather than intimidated, by my power.

I know that my relationship with Christian will be my last because while it's the most sexually fulfilling of my life, it's also the least grounded in the material realm. We fell in love first with each other's spirit, then with each other's mind, then with each other's body.

I think our physical connection is so strong because we didn't give it any power at first. We didn't try to control it or shape ourselves to be who we thought the other would most desire. We just let it happen. We trusted our bodies.

35

I'll never love any beach
as much as Malibu.

About nine months after Christian and I met, we decided to celebrate his fortieth birthday on vacation in Spain. While I had never been to Spain, it held a lot of meaning for Christian, and I couldn't wait to see it through his eyes.

I never thought I'd feel as comfortable in a foreign country as I am in the United States, but I fell in love with the Spanish lifestyle as soon as we started living it—relishing the lively late suppers that wound into the wee hours of the morning, the mandatory afternoon siestas, the unsolicited smiles from strangers on the street. One night at the beginning of our trip, in Barcelona, we decided to pop into a local bingo parlor and play a few rounds. Neither of us speaks Spanish and the calling style there was lightning fast. The bingo parlor was filled with decrepit misfits, and I'm happy to say Christian and I had no problem fitting right in. It reminded me of the rare evening when I get to sneak into the slightly seedy but totally fun Commerce Casino back in LA for a covert session of Celebrity Poker Showdown.

Less than a few games into our bingo adventure, Christian and I had both won jackpots! It seemed like a sign. When we returned home to our hotel that night—romantic and private, the furthest thing from Hollywood fancy—I fantasized about us one day living there together. The service was incredible— we had our own staff of elegant Spanish servants—and we even had a Juliet balcony that looked out on the city. The only thing about the hotel that could have used a little improvement was its name, which was "Casa Fuster." Fuster? How un-*romantico*. Reminded me of "Uncle Fester."

After four nights in Barcelona, we were off to Ibiza. As much as I had loved the city, I was looking forward to the beach, craving the sanity produced by the sound of crashing waves. Christian had suffered a brutal migraine, which resulted in total sleeplessness for both of us our last night in Barcelona, so we felt fragile. Both our bodies were probably filled with dread at the idea of having to leave such a magical city.

I had read thousands of words chronicling the beauty of the hotel in Ibiza where we'd made a reservation, and driving up to the grounds, everything looked appropriately breathtaking. So it came as quite a shock when we entered the room we'd been assigned and it seemed that we'd suddenly been teleported into a Holiday Inn. "I'm not staying here!" I told Christian as I laid eyes on the chintzy floral bedspread that composed the grand centerpiece of our mildewy room. Our room lacked any sense of warmth or character, and even though it was situated on the most beautiful beach in the world, it had no view. Walking out on the patio, which was covered in artificial turf, you could crane your neck past the built-in "private pool" (really a bathtub) and see a sliver of sea.

The patio itself was not private at all. It was on the ground level, visible to people walking around the hotel property. This lack of privacy was the detail that annoyed me most of all; for days, I had been fantasizing about getting naked with Christian on my patio. Funny how such a wish would never have occurred to me before.

Exhausted and resentful, feeling trapped, I embodied that special kind of cranky that comes only with international travel. My mood had turned on a dime; gone was the overwhelming sense of gratitude I'd felt in Barcelona. Now I was back to behaving like a spoiled *Americana* and threatening to start this next leg of our vacation off on the wrong foot.

I wasn't sure I liked this Ibiza place. Where everyone in Barcelona had walked around looking like they'd either jumped off the set of a fashion shoot (wearing avant-garde mullet haircuts and couture jeans) or an old movie (sporting perfectly coordinated skirts and high heels), people on the beach in Ibiza looked—and smelled—like hippies. In Barcelona, people carried Louis Vuitton luggage; in Ibiza, they hoisted knockoff North Face backpacks. Although I am by no means a snob, having biked and schlepped halfway across the world by now, I am the first to admit I love me some luxury.

After taking a second look at our seedy room, just to make sure I wasn't being an unreasonable brat, I decided I didn't care if I seemed spoiled. I wasn't going to let us spend the last part of our perfect vacation in a dump. "I'm sure this isn't your nicest room," I said in my nicest voice over the phone to the front desk.

"That is the room you booked, Madame," replied the attendant crisply. "It is not often our guests are dissatisfied."

I contemplated whether to play the "Do you know who I am?" card. It didn't seem like a solid bet, considering I wasn't sure whether my talk show had ever aired in Spain. If only I could see through the phone line in order to determine whether the reservationist was a John Waters fan. Good indications: feather boa, pencil-thin moustache. Not good: Republican party T-shirt, nonironic trucker hat. "Please let us know when the manager is available to discuss this. We will not be spending our vacation in this depressing room."

We decided to go downstairs and explore the hotel grounds while we were waiting to hear about where they would move us. As underwhelmed as we were by our room, that's how charmed we were by the resort itself.

As we were taking in the scenery, feeling almost comically sorry for ourselves, a beautiful, classy older couple heard us complaining about our room assignment. "You want 509," they said. He looked like a cross between Telly Savalas and Sean Connery; she was an even more beautiful Diane von Fürstenburg. Before they disappeared into the resplendent Ibiza sunshine, the woman told us the location of the best cell reception in the area. Our very own vacation angels.

Meeting with the manager later, we made the request. "That is a very special room," he said. "Let me see whether it is available."

We looked at each other, nervous with anticipation. It's funny how anxious you can get in that moment when you've just found out something very wonderful exists, but you don't yet know whether you'll be able to have it—whether it's a hotel room or true happiness.

"Excellent news," the manager said. "The room is available. It will be 300 additional euros per evening. Is that satisfactory?"

I gulped. As much as I've been blessed with financial success, "an extra 300 euros" is the kind of phrase that gives me hives. I've always been frugal, since every dime I have, I made on my own. And I know what it's like to see money disappear faster than I can earn it. Looking over at Christian, though, this man I loved so completely, I realized that no amount of money was too much to spend on this trip. "We'll take it!" I exclaimed, without that tummy twinge you get when you know you'll regret a purchase.

I had made the right decision. Room 509 was heaven. It had been built into a cliff, overlooking the rest of the hotel, with an incredible view of the beach. This view was accessible from both our huge king-size bed and our own personal—private!—hot tub. Leaning over our massive balcony, we could have jumped right into the pool below. (We didn't, of course. Maybe next time.)

After we unpacked in our incredible new room, and—how shall I say it?—"relieved some of the tension" that had built up over the course of the last day's trip, we got ready to meet Christian's friends at his favorite beach, Las Salinas. Christian had been to Las Salinas Beach for the first time seven years earlier and felt he had been reborn there. Then he'd gone again. This would be his third time, already a charm, and he couldn't wait for me to see it.

I've always been more of a cool, breezy, shoreline-o'-solitude lover than a balmy, oily boogie-down beach fan, so I didn't have high expectations for Las Salinas. I knew there would be DJs spinning house music, and an international crowd, and lots of beautiful people. This all sounded amazing, but I wasn't expecting what sounded like a seaside nightclub to be spiritually transformative. I knew Las Salinas was Christian's thing—I wasn't positive it would also be mine—but I was psyched to go along for the ride.

Getting to Sa Trinxa, the secluded section of Las Salinas that Christian was obsessed with, wasn't easy. We had to drive there from our hotel, park the car, load up all our stuff, then hike almost a mile through deep, white sand, under the hot sun, in order to reach our destination. "Babe, can't we just stop here?" I asked Christian a couple of minutes into our journey.

"Come on, baby," he replied with kindness, encouraging me along. "You'll understand it's worth it when we get there. Sa Trinxa is the best beach. The best."

"Better than Malibu? No way," I asked, then said, answering myself.

"Definitely better than Malibu," Christian replied, with a mischievous glint in his eye. I knew how much Christian loved Malibu, so this was bound to be good. I soldiered on.

As we trekked on, the sand became whiter, the water more and more turquoise. Its color was as saturated and vibrant as the stones that decorated Christian's Indian jewelry. Near the parking lot, I had spotted lots of the sort of people I'd expected to see on vacation in Ibiza: tan, taut kids with huge designer sunglasses wearing bikinis, touching one another in ecstasy, whether real or pharmaceutically manufactured. But as the shoreline we walked along became more remote, we saw a wider range of people in what seemed to be turning into a bohemian paradise. Elderly couples holding hands like newlyweds. Naked hippie families playing paddleball. Teenagers conversing with forty-year-olds enthusiastically in languages I recognized and languages I didn't. It felt like the magical part of the 1960s my parents' generation is always going on about but that my generation isn't entirely convinced ever existed.

I was blown away by the overwhelming spirit of inclusion and acceptance I found at Sa Trinxa. Far from the Eurotrash spring break a tiny part of me was fearing to find there, Sa Trinxa featured a wildly bohemian cast of people from all over the world, of different ages, shapes, and sizes, dancing to their own drummers while grooving to the same beat.

Soon after we arrived at Sa Trinxa, we sat down to have lunch at a little beach restaurant with Ryan, an Irish guy Christian had become very close with when they met in Ibiza years before. Getting to know Ryan myself, I was struck once again by Christian's amazing ability to attract such deep, interesting, compassionate people. Ryan and I clicked immediately.

Christian and I were telling Ryan about my boys—how blessed we were that the three men of the house got along so famously. For a while at that point, Christian and Owen had shared a fixation with those old-timey black mustaches that looked penciled on. Owen would have grown one if he could;

thank goodness, he hadn't yet gone through puberty, so he couldn't have grown a soul patch, much less a mustache. As a substitute, he and Christian often drew little mustaches along the lengths of their ring fingers, which they held up for laughs at opportune moments. It was "their thing," so much so that Christian had promised Owen that he would have a mustache tattooed on his finger in honor of their bond.

"I hope I find it funny forever," Christian told Ryan, laughing. I knew very early on in our relationship that there was nothing Christian wouldn't do for my boys.

"What if you're going to have a ring on your hand at some point?" I asked Christian, emboldened by the sips of sangria I'd had since we sat down to lunch. "Don't you think the tattoo might detract from the ring?" Had I just alluded to us getting married one day? I thought I'd sworn to myself never to get married again! Not to mention, was Christian even interested in getting married to me? All of a sudden, I was acutely aware of my own vulnerability. *Great job, Ricki. Way to ruin your best relationship with meaningless expectations.* What had I done?

I was surprisingly nervous as I waited for Christian to reply. "That's a good point, baby," he said. "I need to decide what to do about this tattoo, but first, we should probably figure out whether I'll be wearing a ring for the rest of my life."

Then my big, handsome man paused for a second, shifting in his chair and leaning toward me.

"Should we do it?" he asked, full of what can be described as nothing other than pure glee. I gasped for air in shock and elation as the man I loved took off his sunglasses, revealing eyes filled with tears. "Will you marry me?"

"YES!" I screamed, like a game show winner, as he grabbed my sweaty, beachy body in his arms. "YES, YES, YES!"

Ryan, who is no doubt a lovely fellow but whom no one would describe as overly emotional, let out a series of huge, wet sniffs. "I'm not crying," he said. "I've got terrible allergies here on the beach!"

Both Christian and I laughed out loud. What an amazing moment that was. We were suspended in this cloud of bliss together, then just flying through the universe hand in hand, fueled by our happiness. Everything felt so right. Never before had it been so clear to me what I wanted. And I was no longer ashamed to want, with every cell of my being.

"Now I have a question for you," Christian said to Ryan, who was still overwhelmed by his "allergies." "Will you be my best man?" Ryan said of course he would, and the two embraced.

I called my friend Jen immediately, the one who had introduced us. "Will you be my maid of honor?" I asked her, hysterical and elated. She screamed "YES!" as well.

After we had shared our joy with Jen, Christian took me by the hand and led me down a long dock, covered in artificial turf, toward the perfect water. "We're taking the plunge together," he said, and we ran toward the water, then jumped in.

Coming up for air, blissfully happy, we noticed all the people around us—lots of beautiful naked young kids, sure, but just as many folks in their fifties, sixties, and seventies, letting their balls and bellies hang out. These were some of the brightest, most interesting people in the world, and this was the beach where they came to really be themselves. The climate of warmth and total acceptance was like nothing I've ever experienced before. Christian embraced me, then took his hands and unstrapped the back of my bathing suit.

Somewhere deep down inside, a little voice was freaking out. *Are you really going to go topless?* it asked. *Are you insane? Have you forgotten what you look like? You don't deserve to show off like that!*

Yes, I do, I replied inside myself, brazen with self-confidence. And in that moment, I actually found myself regretting that I hadn't worn a bikini. Yes, despite my unleashed bosom, I was the only one on that beach in a one-piece. Old habits die hard.

36

I'll never do **Dancing with the Stars.**

When Christian and I returned to the United States after our magical Spanish adventure, I had barely a moment to luxuriate in my newly engaged status before I was faced with having to make a life-changing decision: Should I do *Dancing with the Stars?*

(Yes, I realize calling this a "life-changing" decision is both hyperbolic and hilariously out of touch with the real world, but it is true.)

I'd been asked to be a contestant on the show many times before, and my answer had always been no. I'd already won one dance contest—in *Hairspray*—and that was enough. Why would I subject myself and my body to unbridled criticism from a panel of judges, as well as an audience of millions? I was critical enough of myself; I didn't need to invite others to chime in. And the costume fittings! I shuddered to even think about them. Not to mention that I'd heard the schedule was grueling.

But this time, when faced with the option of appearing on the show, I found myself more intrigued than turned off or terrified. Ever since meeting Christian, I'd felt a renewed sense of enthusiasm when it came to my career. Having his presence as a constant in my life gave me confidence.

It was pretty ironic—here I had finally found a man with whom I never got bored, even after countless hours just lounging and talking—and I was thinking of going back to work. I'd begun developing a new talk show during the few months leading up to our trip to Spain, and it looked as if I'd be returning to syndicated programming the following fall. Yes, I'd vowed long ago never to do another talk show, but this new project would be different from my old one: instead of diving into sensational, sometimes hilarious topics chosen to provoke young people like my old show, this new show would explore in depth the wide variety of things that really mattered to, interested, or mystified me.

I wanted to get into fabulous shape before my new show went into production, but I hadn't been able to pull myself into gear. I'd started more than a few new diets and exercise routines, only to abandon them when Christian told me how hot I looked just the way I was. If I didn't need to lose weight to please him, I damn well was gonna have another piece of pizza. Christian behaved the same way. The first year we were together, we put on a collective 30 pounds. At least the ratio of our mass to each other remained consistent!

But now we had settled into the rhythm of a long-term couple, and I wanted my body back—not for Christian but for myself. And—okay—for Christian too, a little bit. There's nothing more fun than giving someone a present when they haven't asked you for it! And what better way to get into incredible shape than to dance for my life seven days a week? I'd seen my friend Kirstie Alley melt into total hotness, and I knew I could do the same.

⁓

When I began training for *Dancing with the Stars*, I realized that I had a bad habit of always looking down at the floor when I was dancing. I justified this to myself and others by insisting that I needed to monitor what my feet were doing. I didn't like to see myself in the mirror—a reminder that I was not as thin or as pretty as the other girls I was dancing against. My heartbeat quickened every time I saw the girls with perfect bodies at rehearsal, fearing that no matter how hard I tried or how well I danced, my plump physique would never look as good as theirs did on the dance floor.

What a bad habit, always comparing myself to the other dancers. Of course I was proud of myself: I was forty-three years old and on the way to being in the best shape of my life. This was as good as it gets, right? On many levels, I could appreciate how well I was doing considering my body type, training, and ability. Still, it hurt when I wasn't the best.

In order to perform at my own personal best, I needed to fake feeling great about myself. This had always been my survival mechanism. Back when we were making *Hairspray*, I knew I wasn't the best dancer. But I was in every scene, and I was the fat one, and I was the star. I simply *had* to be better than everyone else. As John told me at my audition, it was my job to make the conceit of the film believable—that I was truly the best dancer in Baltimore, despite my size. *Yeah, okay, John—no problem.*

The success of *Hairspray* hinged on the fact that the audience truly believe I was the best dancer of all the kids on *The Corny Collins Show*—white or black, fat or thin. Okay, maybe not black, but definitely white, fat or thin. According to John Waters, I had "natural rhythm." So I wasn't too worried about working with *Hairspray*'s choreographer, the legendary Ed Love. He was going to love me. (Heh, heh.) Ed came to *Hairspray* already a legendary figure in the dance universe, having performed and choreographed on Broadway from a very young age. He was also a member of the Alvin Ailey American Dance Theater, widely considered to be the most gifted and dynamic modern troupe in America, maybe even the world. If I was gonna learn, I was gonna learn from the best.

Going into rehearsals with Ed, I imagined the experience would be as warm and fuzzy as when I'd auditioned for John. Back in that cramped office audition room, as I moved my abundant body to music that played only in my head, I got nothing but positive feedback from John. I loved the smile on his face— the smile that said, "I've finally found the girl I'm looking for." So I walked into my first Ed Love rehearsal sporting the swagger I'd gotten that day.

Flash to one week later. I am shaking like gelatin and covered with sweat, my once heavily lacquered bouffant bangs now plastered to my forehead, rivers of diluted hairspray seeping toxically into my pores.

"Girl, why can't you learn to do the mashed potato? Lord knows you don't need to learn to eat the mashed potato!"

Any swagger I'd once had turned into a slouch.

After Mr. Love had had enough, he turned me over to his assistant, Kiki Shepard, a statuesque African American woman with long legs, big boobs, and no problem doing the mashed potato—or any other dance, for that matter. And she looked like the sort who could eat however much comfort food she wanted without gaining a pound. My body, meanwhile, was my enemy; weighing just over 200 pounds, with tits like footballs and legs like mini–hot dogs, it refused to move as quickly as I wanted it to. Every inch of my physical self was killing me as I tried to meet Ed and Kiki's ridiculous standards. But I pressed on: I wasn't going to squander the first and probably only chance the universe was going to give me to be a star! Every day, Miss Kiki made me repeat the same steps over and over and over again, until I finally got the hang of them (we were nearly done shooting at that point). She cracked the whip too. But she and Ed made me into a dancer. Even though I didn't do so until twenty years later, there was no way I could have done *Dancing with the Stars* without them.

Within five minutes of my starting training with Derek Hough for *Dancing with the Stars,* he was working my ass: hard. Derek teaches with tough love, so it's a good thing I respond well to kind firmness. (Kind firmness works for me not only in rehearsal, of course, but also in more intimate situations. I'll stop there, for the sake of propriety.)

Our first day working together, Derek was charged with teaching me the basics of ballroom. *Let me lead, follow my feet. Keep up with the music. Shoulders down. Eyes up. Check your hold.* Doing what Derek asked me to do was so hard. *Remember this step, kick ball-change! Not on the right foot. Turn on the left!*

Faster, Ricki! Keep up with the music! I felt like a failure at first. What had I been thinking, accepting this gig? I was going to humiliate myself on national television, right before the premiere of my new talk show. Brilliant career strategy, Self.

And then I remembered my fail-safe strategy from the past: fake it 'til you make it. That's what I was going to do.

People often ask me, "How did you gather up the confidence to put yourself out there like that?" My answer may make me sound like an annoying celebrity, but bear with me for a second, because I think what I have to say about this will be relatable even to those who don't live their lives on TV.

As you know, I grew up in front of the camera. Watching myself onscreen for the first time in *Hairspray* was both devastating and exhilarating. It was devastating because I finally had to confront how overweight my body had become, acknowledging the disconnect between how I felt on the inside and how I looked on the outside. But it was also exhilarating because I now had proof that I was capable of achieving what many had seen as an impossible goal: finding success and fame as a freewheeling, lovable fat girl rather than a skinny, self-restricting stick figure.

That I had value just the way I was, even though there were still plenty of things I wanted to change about myself, was a life-altering lesson. Had I not had the confirmation that I mattered when I was still fat, I don't know that I ever would have been able to find the willpower I needed to become thin.

Flash-forward about twenty years after *Hairspray*, to

the time when Christian and I began to fall in love. As I've said already—probably an embarrassing number of times!— Christian and I enjoyed an instantly magical physical chemistry. Sure, I'd had my fair share of great sex before meeting him, but ours was the sort of connection that followed us into and out of the bedroom, the kind of bond that abolishes insecurities and produces an almost hallucinatory sense of calm and well-being.

Falling so quickly into passionate love with each other, we stopped paying attention to our vanities. Lovemaking sessions replaced our daily workouts—excellent calorie burners, sure, had we not followed them with pancakes and milkshakes. Meals taken from the diet delivery cooler were shunned in favor of romantic feasts involving pasta, chocolate, ice cream—we wanted to nourish each other in every way possible.

And nourish each other we did, though we might have overdone it a little bit. As our first-year anniversary approached, Christian and I noticed we'd each put on a bit of weight. For the first time in my life, my reaction to a weight gain was not, *Oh, my God, I look disgusting I'm so weak how did I let this happen now my boyfriend's no longer going to be attracted to me,* but rather, I really want to get back into shape so I can feel better and be the best version of myself for both me and the people I love.

At every single one of my first-week rehearsals, there were two distinct voices in conversation in my head.

You really think you're graceful, Ricki? Nope! You're clutzy. You have two left feet and 25 pounds on any of the professional

*dancers. I can't believe they bedazzled your costume. Did you
really need to call more attention to yourself? You're going to win a
prize, all right: for looking the most like the mirror ball! You have
a show tomorrow, and you're a total mess.*

Part of me was thinking, *You're right, you sadistic little
asshole, you're right.* But I knew that I would never master
the rumba or the cha-cha-cha unless I got that mean voice to
shut the fuck up. So I killed it with confidence. I propelled
myself into the glory of success by living my life in a state of
denial.

When I doubted myself at the beginning of *Dancing with
the Stars,* worrying that I was too fat, too old, too uncoordi-
nated, too irrelevant, I knew I had to counter my inner naysayer with a stream of biased exaggerations, just like I had in
order to learn to dance on *Hairspray* more than two decades
before.

You really think you're graceful, Ricki? Nope! You're clutzy.

Tell that to my hot boyfriend. Oh, and the man who discovered me, the world-famous director, John Waters. Ever heard of
him?

*You have two left feet and 25 pounds on any of the profes-
sional dancers.*

That's not what it says in my Louboutin stilettos. Oh, and
did you know? Muscle weighs more than fat!

*I can't believe they bedazzled your costume. Did you really
need to call more attention to yourself?*

Ballroom dancing getups have to have sequins. It's a rule.
It's in their contract. Just like winning is in mine.

You're going to win a prize, all right: for looking the most like the mirror ball!

You're just jealous because you couldn't win anything if you tried.

One thing I made sure nobody could ever say about me was that I didn't try hard enough.

37

I'll never be the favorite.

❦

Doing *Dancing with the Stars* was more like embarking on a tumultuous new relationship than taking a temporary job. The highs were so high, and the lows were so low. Just like in a new relationship, everything I did was examined under a microscope. And I had to worry not only about one person's impressions and opinions, but also about millions of strangers'. And, of course, my own.

For those who are not familiar with the show's format, here's the basic rundown. Dances, such as the foxtrot or the quickstep, are assigned on Tuesday. Each couple rehearses maniacally all week leading up to the performance show, the following Monday night. On Monday night, each couple performs live in front of a studio and television audience and receives feedback from the judges. Right after the couple finishes their dance, they face the judges' table to listen to their opinions of the dance they've just done.

Getting feedback, the dancers look the judges square in the eye—the camera zooms in on their vulnerable faces as this is happening—as the judges share their impressions. No numerical scores yet, though. For those, the contestants have to run up to the skybox to join all the other couples, so their competitors, along with the live and home audience, can witness the contestants reacting to their marks. (The producers have to milk the shame factor as much as possible.) Getting scores is pretty much always awkward: if you earn better marks than your costars, you feel guilty; if you receive worse, you feel envious. However you feel, everybody knows it.

Also in the skybox, you're interviewed live for the home audience by Brooke Burke-Charvet, the show's drop-dead-gorgeous female cohost, and a past first-place winner back when she was a contestant. Talk about feeling vulnerable, standing next to this brunette Barbie doll wearing a dress that would look like a bathing suit on anyone else. (Worst of all, she's really, really nice!) You're still out of breath and sweaty from the dance you've just performed, and whether you've received great scores or disappointing ones isn't 100 percent clear at the moment. The whole experience is a blur of adrenaline. There's so much going on you can't even really be present to enjoy what's happening.

It was very odd to become so conditioned to being judged by strangers on such a superficial level. In making their assessments of your performance, the judges were literally required to critique our bodies, and our bodies alone: the way they looked, the way they moved, the way they compared to the bodies of others. What a masochistic decision I had made in agreeing to do *Dancing with the Stars*, signing up to be judged so superficially week after week after week, especially since I had struggled with body image issues since the beginning of time. Why had I set myself up for such heartache? I was usually such a positive person.

What was so strange about being put in this uncomfortable psychological position—and what with all the training, physical one too!—was that I was winning. Yes, you read that right: winning.

Week after week, working my ass off with Derek, I earned praise and high scores for my dancing. I was amazed at how my body was able to learn such difficult steps and technique and to grow stronger as I pushed it to its physical limits. Like giving birth, training for *Dancing with the Stars* had turned out to be transformative to me and my relationship with my body—my sense of having a presence in the physical world. Because the dancing is such a purely physical pursuit, it's been a really good lesson for me in terms of getting out of my own way psychologically. There were so many things I did on *Dancing with the Stars* that I never, ever thought I'd be able to do. The show taught me to submit myself to Derek's expertise and to trust that my body would do what he was training it to do.

I was pleasantly surprised by how all our hard work paid off. Soon after the show started, it became clear that J.R. Martinez and I were the contestants to beat. We couldn't have been more different—me, growing up in the spotlight, with an incredible core group of longtime fans and a comfortable life in Los Angeles, and J.R., an Iraq war veteran who had suffered devastating burns on his first tour there, defeated the odds by surviving, and was now enjoying a second career as a motivational speaker and actor. But what J.R. and I shared was a fear-lessness to go for the brass ring and a tirelessness when it came to trying to reach our personal best.

It was a little bit uncomfortable always being neck-and-neck with J.R. for the top spot. I maintained, throughout the process, that he was a better dancer than me—all Latin hips and young-guy swagger. And let us not forget that he was a war hero who had sustained third-degree burns all over his face and body, which put me, and the rest of America, in awe of him.

Week after week, the judges and the home voting audience kept us at the top of the leader board. And after a few confidence-building performances, I started to believe I belonged there. I never really felt like I was the best, but I never felt I deserved to be sent home either.

38

The paparazzi will never care about me.

Walking out of rehearsal each day, covered in sweat, my hair stuck to my face, I could count on being greeted by a handful of grizzly paparazzi screaming my name as I rushed to my car to drive home. "Ricki! Ricki!" It was really insane, all the attention I got as a result of *Dancing with the Stars*. I mean, it's a dance show. Who knew that my appearing on it would mean TMZ would follow me around? I had almost forgotten what it was like to live in the spotlight, and this time around, the scrutiny was crazier than it ever had been.

Paparazzi culture has changed since I was famous the first time. The Internet has made every private moment fair game. I still can't believe people are so interested in keeping tabs on the mundane actions of others, even if they are "famous." And I know it must sound whiny to complain about the inconvenience of encountering a camera or two when I'm on my way to rehearsal or, still sweating, en route to a postshow dinner, what with all the benefits that come with my career, but it's really hard to feel so constantly visible, especially at moments when I feel like I may be falling apart.

I've never been annoyed or frustrated by a real fan coming up to me and asking for an autograph or a hug, but paparazzi have gotten me to reach my boiling point many times. It's the big guys in leather jackets who lurk behind SUVs and lampposts, flashing cameras and microphones in my face when I'm sweating my way home from rehearsal, that really get to me.

Partly because of all the stress that resulted from such intense exposure, I got wrapped up in the competition—losing all sense of reality, in a way. The only thing keeping my feet on the ground, so to speak, was Christian. At the show and at rehearsal, everything was so frantic and frenetic and altogether unreal. But when I came home, into the warm, delicious quiet, ready to savor the downtime I'd been craving all day long, my stress melted away. Nothing felt better than getting home, getting naked, going into the kitchen with the love of my life, and having a snack. It's sort of funny when you think about it: the thing that provided me with the most satisfaction, despite the ridiculously privileged and luxurious life I led, was a moment that has been available to human beings since caveman days. Being naked with my soulmate, sharing a meal. I'm so glad the beauty of such perfect simplicity is not lost on me anymore.

For most of my life, I had been driven by drama—by intense experiences. Now it was finally the simple, even uneventful hours that kept me satisfied. I think it all came down to finally having a sense of safety. To someone who was molested as a child, this was huge because I was actually able to relax and see who I was as a person.

When Christian and I sit in the bath together decompressing—that's a first for me. For me to be completely comfortable, completely naked? That's insane. Normally such a predicament would ensure a visit from the negative voice deep inside me. *What if my fat rolls look as big as my boobs? What if my boobs look droopy? My skin is so white, it's transparent!* It's almost hard to believe I can stand it.

The way Christian relates to my body has nothing to do with what my body actually looks like. Even when we're not wearing any clothes, we can have an incredible conversation that actually means something, and I'm tuned into it, really processing—not pretending to be engaged while actually consumed with self-consciousness about my scars, my stretch marks, the size of my thighs. Finally, I've broken down an important barrier in this relationship: I'm able to accept being unconditionally loved. And I think Christian feels the same way.

Don't get me wrong, it's not like our lives are perfect. Every couple deals with shit of some kind or another. For some reason, people are obsessed with the discrepancy between my financial worth and Christian's—as though the fact that he's not rich means he must be out to take advantage of me. I wonder, when people warn their friends about their suspicion that their significant other might be a gold digger, do they not realize they are profoundly insulting the person they are claiming to try to protect? What a friend is really saying when she says your boyfriend is only in a relationship with you for the money is, "Hey, pal, I hate to be the one to break this to you, but you know you couldn't possibly be appealing for anything other than your money, right?" Not to mention the fact that anyone who accuses Christian of being financially opportunistic just doesn't know him. He couldn't care less about material wealth. He grew up in his family business of trading southwestern and Native American jewelry—he's actually experienced the barter system firsthand—and he feels most at home when he's out in nature, not at some fancy hotel. Finally, I wanted to ask the haters, *Haven't I proven by now that I am capable of taking care of my-self? After all the harm I've defended myself against, does it really make sense that I would choose to spend my life with someone who's taking advantage of me?*

I can't imagine a better person for me to end up with than Christian. The bottom line is, in terms of a man, I *don't* need material wealth. Isn't that so obvious? As someone who's led a financially lucrative career, I have the luxury of choosing a man based solely on who he is. And that's something money can't buy.

It's the ups and downs that make a good story, and television producers—even the ones working on reality shows—know this. They engineer their programs to lead viewers one way, then switch things up completely and have them believing something else entirely. It may be somewhat manipulative, but it makes good television. I, of all people, should know.

Although I worked my ass off all through my season of *Dancing with the Stars* and I believe that I improved consistently from week to week, I fell out of favor with the judges from time to time. Sometimes they'd criticize my technique, sometimes my musicality—and while I agreed with some of their criticisms, a lot of the time I did not. The scoring system seemed inconsistent sometimes, and even though I always knew I could do better, I'm not going to pretend it didn't get frustrating.

Because all the contestants were literally pitted against one another, dealing with some elements of the *DWTS* competition wasn't easy, especially as the group of people competing became relatively small. When you spend so much time with a small group of people hoping to accomplish the same task—in our case, getting really good at ballroom dancing over a ridiculously short period of time—bonding is inevitable. But eventually so is a bit of infighting, resentment, and jealousy. Competition can reveal people's personal best, but it can also bring out their worst—and there's nothing that disappoints me more than re-alizing I had someone's true colors all wrong. I can't help but be honest all the time, wearing my heart on my sleeve. Even though I've been on this earth for forty-three years, I'm so naive that every time someone I get close to turns out to be two-faced, I'm shocked. Please do not think I'm trying to take any moral high ground here—I wish I were capable of being sneakier, of concealing my motives—but I'm incapable of acting like a con-vincing phony, and it never ceases to amaze me when people I think I know well turn out to be acting their way through real life.

I hate the idea of living in a world where everything I say and do is calculated rather than natural. Performing your way through life is exhausting and no fun at all. Even though I just recently decided to get back into television for the first time in more than a decade, I'm already fantasizing about the change in lifestyle I'll experience when my kids fly the nest for college and Christian and I can leave LA. I can really see us taking a different turn—finding our way out of "the business," living a simple life—and not one recorded for a reality show.

The format of the show created really uncomfortable group dynamics too. On one occasion, just after we'd all received our scores, we found out that we'd be divided into two teams of three couples each in order to learn and perform a group dance. Because J.R. and I had earned the highest overall scores of the night, we were designated the team captains for the group dance competition. Immediately I knew what we were going to have to do, and my heart pounded even thinking about it: we were going to have to pick teams, just like in gym class.

I was instantly transported back to elementary school. My face flushed with the anxiety of worrying about being chosen, of having to choose. There was no question in my mind which was worse. What was truly horrible was being in control, being forced into a position in which I would have to hurt somebody's feelings.

Former fat kids always talk about the anguish of being the pariahs of PE class, and I understand all too well the humiliation of being the last one picked. By and large, though, despite my childhood chubbiness, people were happy to have me on their team. I was a cuddly, people-pleasing mascot and, in spite of my weight issues, not too bad at sports. Even back then, though, I had a stronger aversion to other people's pain than to my own. I never wanted to be team captain, capable of making other kids feel small.

That team-choosing day in the skybox, we did a coin toss to determine whether J.R. or I would choose first. I won, and immediately threw all the responsibility of team picking onto Derek's shoulders. "It's up to you," I told him, on camera. "I don't even want to participate." Derek was happy to jump in—he's a genius and cares as much about strategy as choreography and performance—and his smart recruitment decisions scored us the winning team. But I was beyond relieved not to have to make anyone feel bad about themselves. I wouldn't have minded if our team had lost as long as I'd escaped hurting my fellow dancers' feelings.

39

I'll never throw in the towel.

At the midpoint of my time on *Dancing with the Stars*, I was totally depleted. Emotionally, I felt that I had no more to give. Derek never took it easy on me. He would work my ass, just like Ed and Kiki did. Never giving up when I couldn't seem to get a step, Derek would push and push and push—sometimes to the point where he became so frustrated, he yelled at me, even as I was on the verge of collapsing from exhaustion. There were days when, even after I'd learned a lot and significantly improved my technique, Derek actually got angry at me. We weren't always the don't-go-to-bed-angry types (in our case, "going to bed" meant leaving rehearsal). Sometimes we'd part ways raging at each other. Instead of feeling resentful of Derek for pushing me to my limit, I felt guilty about disappointing him. Later, he told me that he'd learned being harsh with me would get him much better results than giving positive feedback. Hearing this made me sad, but I had to admit that it made sense given the patterns I'd grown up with.

I always felt a tiny bit guilty for being partnered with Derek—like I wasn't glamorous enough or tiny enough. In the past, he'd been partnered with Brooke Burke, Nicole Scherzinger, and Jennifer Grey—all teeny-weeny starlets (and incidentally, all first-place winners). In comparison to them, I saw myself as a dancing hippo. Derek is basically a living, breathing Ken doll—5'10" and 100 percent muscle, with boyish blond hair and blue eyes. Being around someone who has achieved his level of physical perfection—not just being *around* him but being *face-to-face* with him, everything *touching*, lips and eyes just an inch apart—made me feel really insecure.

As I'm sure anyone who weighs a pound over 125 can imagine, my entire body shook with anxiety the week I found out we had reached the stage of the competition where all couples were going to be required to start doing lifts. At this point, I'd already lost about 15 pounds, which was incredible. Everyone was shocked by the changes in my body over just seven weeks—no one more than I. But although I knew objectively how much less space my body was taking up, I was terrified Derek wouldn't be able to lift me or, worse, that he'd hurt himself trying—and then everyone in the world would watch my cheeks flush with the redness of shame, the burning ardor of complete embarrassment.

Part of the guilt that comes with being fat is that you know you're putting undue strain on the people you love if you ask them to carry your weight around—both emotionally and physically. So you isolate yourself, tell yourself you're just "independent," when what you really are is afraid of overwhelming others with your weight and worrying they might drop you.

40

I'll never feel as good as I did giving birth.

⁓

I've said many times that I first began to truly accept my body after giving birth to my son, Owen, at home in my New York bathtub. Seeing what my physical self was capable of—nothing less than shepherding new life into the world—revealed my superficial concerns and criticisms about lumps, bumps, and stretch marks for what they truly were. Before this life-changing event, if you'd asked me whether I'd agree to appear naked in a documentary destined to be viewed by millions of people— many of whom I knew!—I would have said, "No fucking way." But years after Owen was born, I included footage of his birth, which consisted of images of me in labor and delivery, totally nude, in my film about childbirth choices, *The Business of Being Born*. I was wholly unprepared for the backlash that resulted.

From *CBS News:*

Now another B-list celebrity is pushing the child-exploitation envelope to the limit. In what looks to me like a blatant bid to escape the where-are-they-now file, Ricki Lake is releasing video of her naked in a bathtub giving birth. No, it's not a new title for the fetish aisle of your local adult movie outlet. She's the executive producer of a critical documentary ironically titled, *The Business of Being Born.* In an interview with *Huffington Post,* Lake claims she filmed the birth of her second son for her own personal record and never intended to show the video to the public. Right. I'm guessing whoever was behind the camera was thinking, "movie career revival—kaching!" (The documentary is featured at the Tribeca Film Festival this month. I'll be watching for the faked, post-partum reverse shots of a wide-eyed daddy waiting for his son to pop out.)

To be fair, the writer of this piece, Mario Wuebben, followed up with another one after he'd actually seen the movie, titled "I Saw Ricki Lake Naked—and Liked It." In it, he admits to having gotten a lot out of our movie and wraps up the piece with, "Yes, Ricki Lake bares all. But it's completely nonsexual—like a nude beach at a senior center. And I really liked it." A nice apology, but also, of course, missing the point completely.

From *Seattle Weekly:*

Most of the advance buzz about *The Business of Being Born* has centered around an image of its producer, Ricki Lake. Naked. Giving birth. In a bathtub. If you couldn't handle the crowning scene in *Knocked Up*, you should probably pass on this one; not only is Lake's real labor about a million times more explicit (she flops and writhes for a long while, then a gunk-covered infant slowly emerges from between her legs), but we see quite a few other women popping out babies as well, in every imaginable contortion. Even the director, Abby Epstein, joins the club, turning the camera on her own attempt at natural childbirth for her doc about the birthing biz.

And finally, from TMZ:

"I am naked at 195 pounds giving birth in my own bathtub," Lake recently told *The Huffington Post*. "It can't get any more intimate than that!" And it shouldn't.

"And it shouldn't?" *Who the hell do you think you are to decide?*

I vowed not to let myself get too upset, refusing to let this absurdly superficial criticism damage my own self-image. In order to do this, I had to come to terms with a few sad truths about our society. Why, I asked myself, do we have such a hard time looking at the ripe, unclothed female body when it's the source of all human life? Because we are so conditioned to present a false mask of feminine "perfection" to the world that a long hard look at a real woman in labor—a woman who has not undergone a Photoshop intervention or been fitted with a prosthetic belly to hide behind—appears almost grotesque. I was shocked by the number of anonymous everywomen all over the Internet condemning my decision to appear in the film un-clothed. I had to assume that some women become so ashamed of their own changing flesh during pregnancy that they view women who choose to share images of their pregnant bodies as suspect—even threatening—and feel the need to speak out against them in order to protect themselves, in order not to be forced to question the choices they make in their own lives.

After this trying time, I swore I'd never be so hard on my-self again. I agreed not to separate my physical and emotional selves, and whenever I had the urge to rip my body to shreds, I vowed to always consider the incredibly generous and magi-cal things my body had done for me. But time passes, and, like everyone else, I suppose, I forgot about the promises I'd made to myself. As my boys grew up and my birthing days trailed long behind me, I strayed back to the superficial. Every day I received a delivery of a cooler full of diet food, little plastic containers filled with munchkin portions that were supposed to nourish me, body and soul. Each day I beat myself up for not eating them. I kept an ear out for the latest and greatest in weight-loss schemes and kept a careful mental inventory of how much space there was between my ass and the waistband of my size-eight jeans.

Until I met Christian, my self-image when it came to my weight was a real roller-coaster ride—and even I didn't know when to prepare for the loop-de-loops and drops. My self-esteem was directly tied to how attractive I felt and how attractive I felt was determined by all things physical: *How did my jeans fit today versus yesterday? How would a man who'd never before seen me*

in his entire life describe me to his friends: as "cute," "hot," "fat,"
"voluptuous," or with a "rockin' bod"? Would someone just meet-
ing me know I'd ever had a weight problem or assume I didn't
know what it meant to struggle with the scale—that I'd been born
one of the lucky ones?

Even though Christian always made me feel like his love for me went far deeper than my skin, I brought some of these neurotic questions into our relationship. I remember, after my first week on *Dancing with the Stars*, when I'd already whittled off a fairly astounding number of inches but was still struggling to lose the weight I'd allowed to creep on in the early stages of our romance, Christian and I were sitting opposite each other in my huge porcelain bathtub. Looking straight ahead, I saw my tiny toes floating on the surface of the water, nails painted red and covered in bubbles, and then just beyond them, Christian's warm, handsome, honest face. His eyes looked at my nude body with total acceptance. There was no reason to think I was any-thing less—or more—than everything this incredible man had ever wanted. And yet I was still plagued by self-doubt.

41

*I'll never find someone who loves
me the same, fat or thin.*

"Can you believe I lost eight-and-a-half inches already, baby?"
I asked Christian just a little over halfway through my time
on *Dancing with the Stars*. I could hear the vulnerability shake
through my own voice. My man smiled back at me with sweet en-
couragement, but he didn't say a word in reply. For no logical reason, I felt a little bit nervous about his silence. Maybe he hadn't
heard me? I dialed up my volume. "Do you prefer me smaller?"
I continued, trying to elicit a response. He just smiled. Still said
nothing. I kept prodding. "Or do you even have a preference?"

I couldn't believe I insisted on articulating this question so
clearly, leaving myself so open to pain, pressing him to answer
me. *Maybe I should take the hint and let him demur. Maybe he's
trying to protect my feelings.*

What if his answer were yes? What if I made him say it out loud? Would I then worry for the rest of my life that every time I gained a pound or two I'd made myself repellent to him? Why wasn't he saying anything?

Sensing my neurosis, Christian laughed kindly but still offered no opinion. But I wanted an answer. "Are you more attracted to me now that I'm smaller?" I asked, my voice—and heart rate—speeding up. I barely waited for him to open his mouth before continuing, "You don't care at all? You don't have a preference? Really?"

Finally, Christian broke his silence and, squeezing my feet, said, "I just want you to be happy with your body, Ricki. I love you no matter what size you are."

Sweet relief washed over me, and truthfully, I felt a tiny bit silly. Had I really doubted that he felt that way? As I thought about it, I realized that in repeating my question over and over again, I was really asking myself, not Christian, whether the bigger version of me was worth less than the smaller one. It was time for me to acknowledge how judgmental I was—and had always been—about my own weight. Sure, there had been scores of people over the course of my life who had judged me, unfairly, for it, but the most critical voice had always been my own.

Thankfully, when pressed, the man I'd chosen to spend the rest of my life with answered "correctly," even though I hadn't realized that I was testing him.

Before me, Christian had been with mostly skinny women. Since the first time we got physical, I was curious about which kind of female body he thought felt better pressed up against his—one finessed by its curves or defined by its angles. My curiosity must have stemmed at least in part from my own long-held insecurities. But I've also always been interested in learning about a man's pure response to a woman's physical being, separate from what society has conditioned him to feel. While entertainment and media dictate that men should prefer slim, lithe silhouettes, many guys say that nothing beats some well-placed adipose tissue in the bedroom.

But there's a difference between a baby who's got back, and one who gets back at you—by eating themselves into a shame spiral. And so I certainly understand how some men—and women too—express a sense of disappointment or even embarrassment when their partners put on weight. It's hard not to see your partner as a reflection of yourself, especially when you also struggle with weight issues.

Years ago we tackled this issue on my talk show. The topic was, "What happens when your partner gains a lot of weight?" As I'm sure you can imagine, the reactions this question provoked were passionate. Audience opinions were split pretty much down the middle of the issue, with one side of the room saying, "It's what's on the inside that counts, and if you don't agree, you're a shallow asshole!" while the other replied, "Let's get real. You have to be attracted to someone to stay in love with them, and when someone doesn't take care of their body, it's a sign they no longer respect the relationship. They might as well wear a T-shirt that says, 'FUCK YOU.'"

Of course I know that the inside is what matters, but I relate to both sides of the argument. Weight gain can become a serious problem between two people when it reflects a shift in one member's priorities—away from the couple's physical connection or health.

Until I met Christian, I looked to date men who, simply by appearing next to me in pictures, would validate my own attractiveness and desirability. I felt okay about myself as long as I was able to attract a certain type of guy. During what I now refer to as my rock-bottom-feeders period, I rarely experienced true emotional or physical intimacy. I think the explanation for this was simple: I had run out of emotional space. My father had been really sick, and my mother had left him at his weakest moment. I hated her; he needed me. And so did my little boys, and to a certain extent, so did their dad, even though we hadn't been together in that way for a long, long time. There simply wasn't enough of me left over for a real relationship, so I filled my dance card with insignificant men.

Thank goodness, I was just going through a stage. When I realized that I would rather sleep in my giant bed alone every night than lie next to any of the guys I'd dated in the past few months, I finally said to myself, "I'm tired of eating dinner with idiots and having casual sex. I'm tired of hiding the fact that I'm a fully developed, emotionally complex woman who needs a real man, not some Hollywood dude stuck in a state of perpetual adolescence."

I started seeing a genius therapist named Lisa, who made me realize that I needed to value my own long-term happiness more than the disconnected mini-relationships I was having with various good-looking yet highly inappropriate men. I decided to ask myself what sort of man I really wanted in my life instead of trying to pursue one who would make me appear "happy" and "lucky" from the outside. I had to make peace with

the fact that I would not be happy with an egomaniacal pow-
erhouse who viewed his career as more important than mine
or feel "lucky" to settle for an easygoing pretty boy who lacked
emotional depth.

I resigned myself to being single for a long, long time—
if not forever. Spending time alone, I realized that I had never
truly wanted what my family and our society had always told
me I was supposed to want. I didn't need some guy with a
great career and tons of money to support me. I already lived
in a multimillion-dollar house that I had paid for in cash with
money I'd earned myself. I'd never been romantically motivated
by a man's success. In fact, men who put earning money above
all else had always been a turn-off to me. I was an alpha woman
who craved a beta male—someone who supported me emotionally rather than financially. I found that when I found Christian.

42

I'll never meet a man who's totally comfortable in a room full of women.

The first time my friend Amy met Christian, we were all attending a birthing event—the sort of get-together many of us lovingly refer to as a "vagina rally." Not exactly the most comfortable place for a man to hang out, to put it mildly, but Christian was unfazed. Amy noticed him from across the room, where he was playing quietly with my younger son, Owen. They were lying on the floor together, wearing hula skirts, without a care in the world. Amy looked at me, pointed at Christian and Owen, and mouthed, "Perfect." I knew she was right. This man was perfect for me. This man was perfect for my children. This man was—perfect.

Every moment we were together, I fell more in love with his gentle soul, and it warmed my heart that the people I loved noticed how wonderful a man I had found.

The kind of symbiotic relationship Christian and I have together is rare. I don't think there are many men like him. With him, I feel taken care of and supported. He's very sure of himself and has a strong sense of personal morality. There's not a phony bone in his body. He radiates sensitive, intense, authentic energy, which almost seems female in the most beautiful way possible. We laugh about it, calling him a lesbian. At the same time, though, there's no doubting he's a real man. If you know what I mean.

Every other man I've been with has felt threatened by my successes, but not Christian. He gets true pleasure out of seeing me rise and achieve my goals. We joke that right now, his career is being there for me, but he doesn't look at that job as mattering less than any other, and neither do I, mostly because he takes such pride in seeing me blossom. I'm okay with that. I don't need him to pull in a paycheck.

We often joke about the time I broke my toe and was in sheer agony unless he did everything for me. If he could have walked for me, I would have let him. He replied, "I'll always take care of you, baby," each time I thanked him for being so kind.

"I'll always hire the best to take care of you, baby," I'd respond. This is a relationship between two people who really know who they are.

Christian and I, despite being so different from each other, share some profound things in common. The most important is the way both of us grew up deriving strength and inspiration from our grandparents. My Grandma Sylvia and Grandpa

Alvin were married for forty years, spending every one of them madly in love with each other. He died when she died basically; although Alvin remained on this earth longer than Sylvia did, he was never the same without her. Christian's grandparents were the same way. Although Christian and I both grew up with parents who suffered from serious marital problems, we were able to see past these tragic relationships and knew that real love was possible. It had just skipped a generation.

One thing Christian learned from his grandpa was not to hold a grudge—no argument is worth wagering a relationship over. "Don't go to bed angry," Christian's grandpa always told him, and he was right. In my first marriage, I thought I'd be doing everybody a favor if I kept my unhappiness to myself, straining to contain it until I just couldn't bear the pressure anymore. Now I know that I couldn't have been more off base. Honesty is at the very core of my relationship with Christian. I still like to be right all the time, of course (who doesn't?), but I feel and behave differently now. In the way Christian and I interact, there's not an ounce of me putting on a show for him or doing something I don't want to do because I think he wants me to do it. I also find myself thinking about his feelings a lot, with every move I make. I know that my behavior affects not only me and my happiness, but his as well. This may sound obvious, but I didn't used to pay much attention to other people's feelings when it came to achieving my goals. *It's my life, and I'll do what I want,* I thought. Now I realize that my self-centered point of view developed because I didn't grow up knowing a woman was supposed to support her man emotionally. My own mother provided me no model.

I'm so happy now to be in a healthy relationship. I'd forgotten how much I love representing half of a couple. I didn't think being not single was important to me, but it's really nice not to have to do anything alone—to have a partner who is nurturing and whose love is unconditional. Christian is precious to me in so many ways. After my divorce from Rob, I never dreamed I'd again love someone enough to build a life around him.

Neither Christian nor I had the childhood we deserved. He grew up mostly worrying about the happiness and safety of his young, single mom, and I felt varying degrees of distance from my parents and my sister. I'm sure my dad always loved me unconditionally, but because of the chilly climate my mother cultivated in our home, that wasn't always clear. Because of how difficult our own childhoods were, Christian and I decided not to have children together. Since we each had to grow up so fast, we wanted to be there for each other's inner child instead of an imaginary real one.

Now that I'm with Christian, I've never felt so taken care of. I feel even safer than when I was a child, though in my case, that's not really saying much. Even more than when I was a child. When I need to cry, he holds me and lets me let loose. I feel safe, nurtured, and loved unconditionally. It's like Christian is making up for all the time I wasn't taken care of. He truly fills a void I didn't know I had. I had become so hardened, but he's blown the protective shell right off me. I'm a believer in love again.

43

*My ex-husband and my boyfriend
will never get along.*

⁓

Christian incorporated himself into the daily life of me and my boys with total effortlessness. I loved waking up next to him in the morning, warmed by the body heat of both my dog, Jeffie, and his dog, Pacha. The boys begged him, not me, to take them to school and soccer games. We started having family dinners— a cozy, intimate daily wrap-up neither Christian nor I had ever really had growing up.

The one thing that made me nervous about my new family situation was the tension that seemed inherent to my boys growing up with two father figures. I had been through a very difficult time with their dad, Rob, but I still held him in high regard, and it was important to me that he always be a strong presence in my boys' lives.

Christian, the man with whom I would live the rest of my life, deserved to be acknowledged by the boys as a father figure of a different sort, but I was worried that by showing him their love, the boys would worry about seeming disloyal to Rob. How would the boys be able to negotiate space in their hearts and lives for both men? Was I a bad mother for putting them in this situation? How could I worry about that, given that all I'd done was increase the amount of love and support in their lives? How could we all be in the same room at the same time without my suffering an anxiety attack?

Difficult as honing these new family dynamics sounded, I knew the job was one I'd have to do alone. I didn't want to put any pressure on my kids or make them divide their loyalties. I wanted them to feel lucky about having a blended and extended family. Ever since Christian and I had gotten together, I'd taken pleasure in watching him interact with Milo and Owen, whether helping them build a massive trampoline in our yard, taking them for cool haircuts, or picking them up from school.

Still, every mother leading her children through divorce has so many worries. Worries that the sadness and separation will squelch their childlike joy. Worries that their authentic personalities could be suppressed because of loyalty to one parent or another. Worries that no matter how hard she tries to create a nurturing home environment, her children will always blame her for letting their "real" family break apart. It was important to me that the boys be able to love both Christian and Rob, without fear of hurting one or the other's feelings. And it was crucial that Christian and Rob get along. How could I be sure?

I had to make peace with the fact that I couldn't control the universe, and I calmed myself by realizing that Christian and

Rob were unlikely ever to be in the same place at the same time. I didn't have to know all the answers yet. We could just figure things out as we went along.

Well, the universe has a way of expediting outcomes.

About eleven months after Christian and I had been together and just a couple of weeks after we had gotten engaged, the boys needed to be picked up from summer camp. I had planned to do the pickup myself, but my schedule was tight. So the plan was for Christian and me to drive to the bus stop together and meet the kids. Then I'd jump in a chauffeured car to head south to San Diego, to speak at a women's Internet conference, while Christian would drive the boys home to Brentwood.

The boys' bus ended up being late, and I had to head off before they arrived. I was so bummed. When your kids have been gone for a month, there's nothing better than seeing those smiling, tan faces glowing with pride. Christian stayed at the bus stop to meet the boys. At this point, he had been living with us for a good six months, so the boys would find it perfectly normal to see him waiting there.

I knew that their father would be waiting there too, but I could never have anticipated what would happen next.

On my drive to San Diego, Christian told me as I spoke to him on the phone, that he and Rob had been talking, hanging out while waiting for the boys.

"Since you and I are planning to tell the boys about our engagement when you get home, I decided to tell Rob about it. I thought he deserved to know before they did. I didn't want him to be blindsided."

I was speechless.

"So while we were waiting for the boys' bus to come, I said, 'Rob, I want to share some news with you. Ricki and I just got engaged in Ibiza. We are going to be getting married next year. And I want you to know that I am not only committing to Ricki but also to your boys.'"

"And?" I asked, dying to know how Rob had reacted, nearly jumping out of my skin at the prospect of Rob and Christian hanging out together by the side of the road, with no members of my gene pool in sight to justify their bizarre pairing. The image was simultaneously horrifying and comforting. "Well, what did Rob say?"

"Rob was great!" Christian said. "He said, 'Thank you so much for telling me. I'm really happy for you both. I know the boys love you, so please tell them I'm completely on board.'"

"Wow!" I yelped, truly speechless. I was flabbergasted and overwhelmed with gratitude. How had I come to have such incredible people in my life? It was such a pleasure to hear that the best part of Rob had been reawakened—that the generous and kind man I had once fallen in love with had chosen to show himself to the new man in my life. I felt lucky Christian had been let in on that side of him and so blessed to be in love with a man so secure in himself. Although my relationship with Rob is damaged as a result of the breakup of our marriage, I know he still wants me to be happy. And though I was thrilled that Rob and Christian had shared their own special moment, I was truthfully a little bit envious and devastated to miss it. I want to be everywhere all the time, but I can't.

Christian told me that when Milo and Owen ran off the bus from camp, they saw him talking with Rob, and the two boys ran up to the two men together, unable to mask their happiness.

Christian saw no reason to break up the party, so he suggested the four of them go to Fatburger for lunch, then hang out back at our house to tell camp stories. The boys didn't want to choose cars, so they flipped a coin to see who'd ride with whom, and then they drove in a little caravan.

I got back to the house from my event in San Diego at 10:30 that evening. Milo was still awake. Tan and lean at age fourteen, with short hair and a wry smile, he looked on his way to being a grown-up. I was so proud of him.

"I have some news," I said to Milo, nervous. I knew he'd had such a wonderful day, and I didn't want to risk ruining it. I didn't really know how he felt about me and Christian; still, the universe seemed to be favoring us that day, so I found the courage to continue. "Christian and I are going to get married."

"Really?" he asked, with a much bigger smile than I could have hoped for.

"Really!" I said.

"Are you going to have a wedding?" he asked. Why would he ask such a thing? I wondered. I could only imagine it was because he was worried that his father might feel left out.

"I want you to know that Daddy is completely supportive."

My big boy smiled at me with what I think was gratitude. It's so easy to forget how sensitive boys are since they hold everything so deep inside.

Milo and I went in to tell his little brother the good news. "Owen!" I whispered, as Milo and I creeped into his room. "How was camp?"

"Great!" he said in his sleepy, gravelly, yet totally enthusiastic little voice.

"I'm so happy to see you!" I said as I hugged him. His little arms were wrapped around Cher, a tattered stuffed frog who goes with him everywhere. She is more brown than green, and wears a teeny-tiny T-shirt with a photo of baby Milo printed on it. Pretty much the most charming security blanket—er, amphibian—in the world.

"I'm so happy to see you too," he replied groggily.

"I have some news for you if you're awake."

"I'm awake! I'm awake!" He sat up in bed and rubbed his eyes. "What is it?"

"Christian and I are engaged," I said in a happy whisper.

"Wow!" Owen said. "That's great!" Then he paused for a moment, excited. "Mom! Mom! You know what else?"

"No, honey—what else?"

"Dad and Christian are really good friends now too!" Even Cher seemed animated by Owen's happiness.

I was so touched to see how much that meant to him.

But I was amazed to see how much it meant to me.

The night of the *Dancing with the Stars* finale, the studio was lit up like a Christmas tree, and the sequins I was decked out in made me sparkle like an ornament. I couldn't believe how much my body had changed through the course of the show, but even more, I couldn't believe the changes in my mind.

For the first time, I was valuing process just as much as product. I enjoyed learning each new dance just as much as I enjoyed earning high marks. I was happy to be growing—and shrinking!—as a dancer, not devastated each time I failed to be perfect.

Over the past few weeks, I'd been pretty proud of my own performance, and I could feel people across the country rooting for me. I worked hard and I'm an okay dancer, but I think my success tapped into a deep sense of wish fulfillment for everyone who has ever felt trapped by his or her body. Who would have thought that the chubby girl would be the last woman standing in a ballroom dancing competition?

The other two finalists were J.R. Martinez, the war hero with serious natural rhythm, and Rob Kardashian, the dark horse with an insane fan following. I liked both of them very much and was happy just to be reaching the end of the season. My body was tired.

Of course I wanted to win, and for a while, I believed that I might. But by the time we taped the finale, I knew I wouldn't take first place, and I had a strong sense I'd come in third.

My hunch was pretty much confirmed when I saw where the producers had seated my family and guests, at a round table slightly removed from the dance floor and in front of a bunch of camera equipment. More than once before the show started, my friends were warned not to stand up to cheer for me, so as not to block any shots. Rob and J.R.'s respective crews were practically smashed up against one another for dramatic effect (and easy camerawork) in the very front row along the length of the stage.

The way the finale was structured, the top three dancers would start the show, then one would be eliminated, and the top two would be revealed around the midpoint. Then the top two couples would be judged on the way they danced an "instant samba," for which they would be able to prepare for just a few minutes during the live taping of the show.

I knew that if Derek and I made it to the last competition

round, we'd have a good chance. Both of us are excellent under pressure, and we thrive on the energy of a crowd. Most important, my samba dress was a real killer, and I wanted to wear it. But even before the night started, I knew that I wouldn't get to.

My intuition had been correct. I had prepared myself to be disappointed, and I was right. I appreciated the crowd's gasp when Tom and Brooke announced I'd been eliminated, but I was ready for it.

During the break at the midpoint of the show, the producers told me I'd get to sit in the audience to watch the action rather than try to sneak a peek from backstage, where I'd been trapped all season. I was so excited to join my family—my boys, Christian, Marie, and a few of my closest friends—and to celebrate the end of my journey. I wanted them to know that I was the furthest thing from sad, that I was proud of myself, and ready to sit back and relax for the first time in months.

But when I ran onto the floor to join Christian and my boys, the producers grabbed me away and told me I had to sit on the other side of the stage, in between the Kardashians and J.R.'s family. They almost had to pull me from Christian physically— I wanted to be with him so badly, and I could tell he wanted to comfort me about my loss. I needed to reassure him that I was okay.

I was a little bit lonely sandwiched between the two winning entourages, but the hidden perk of my seat assignment was that it gave me a perfect view of my home team. There was Milo, my firstborn, looking more man than boy with his close-cropped hair and dapper suit. There was Owen, whose big, expressive eyes reminded me so much of my own. And there was Christian, my man, supporting me with every handsome inch of himself. It moved me to see him there with my boys, like all the time I'd spent feeling so alone in my life had really added up to something.

Back when I was eighteen, I danced in *Hairspray* as if my life depended on it. And it did. I was looking desperately for a way out of a life I didn't fit into. But no longer. Now I looked into the audience at the faces of the people who loved me, fat or thin, winner or loser, and I realized this was what I had been searching for all along: a life I didn't have to try to squeeze myself into. A life made to fit me.

Acknowledgments

The reason I decided not to have a big wedding was to avoid the anxiety and pressure of coming up with a guest list. My publishers, however, wouldn't let me out of writing these acknowledgments—and for that, I'm grateful. The following people deserve my warmest thanks for their invaluable help with this book:

Rebecca DiLiberto, for being my sister from another mother. I couldn't have done this without you.

John Waters, for striking the perfect balance between fairy godmother and Hollywood dad. I am so grateful that you chose me.

Howard Borris, for keeping me out of trouble for twenty-two years and counting. You are my surrogate father, and I love you.

Andy McNicol at WME, for convincing me that now was the time to tell my story.

Sarah Durand at Simon & Schuster, for offering my book a wonderful home.

Josh Sabarra, for truly understanding who I am and helping everyone else get me, too—"With you for me and me for you, we'll muddle through, whatever we do!"

Nancy Josephson, for being such a supporter of mine after all these years.

Caroline Ellett, I don't know how you keep all the balls in the air—thanks y'all!

There is a group of people who've played such important roles in my life, that without them there'd be no story to tell. They are: Abby, Ana Paula, Belinda, Camryn, Chia Julie, Frances, Geoff, Howard Bragman, Iris, Jack, Jen M., Lisa, Lynn, Marie, Molly, Pammy, Paulo, Rachael, Rob, Robin, Simon, and Thea. And, of course, Barry, Jennifer, and Jill Lake. Once again, I want to thank Christian Evans, who changed the course of this book, and gave me my happy ending.

Most of all, I want to thank my boys, Milo and Owen, for helping me find my life's truest purpose: being their mom.

Nobody puts my feelings for all of these incredible people into words better than my friend, the brilliant lyricist and composer Lance Horne: "What matters are the things I've learned from you, and the rough and tumble way in which we grew, and the time it takes to love another truly true."

I'll never be more grateful to all of you than I am right now.

—Ricki

Oh! Wait! Even though this list is long, I'm sure I've forgotten someone. If this person is you, please accept my apologies and refer to Chapter 26, which tells the story of my struggle with Ambien amnesia.